Bulbs and Tubers

KLAAS NOORDHUIS AND SAM BENVIE

FIREFLY BOOKS

Cataloguing in Publication Data

Noordhuis, Klaas T.
Bulbs and tubers : the complete guide to flowers from bulbs

(The gardener's library)
Includes index.

ISBN 1-55209-202-X

1. Bulbs. I. Benvie, Sam. II. Title.
III. Series: The gardener's library (Toronto, Ont.).

SB425.N66 1998a 635.9'4 C97-931994-3

Published in the United States in 1998 by
Firefly Books (U.S.) Inc.
P.O. Box 1338
Ellicot Station
Buffalo, NY USA
14205

Design and layout: *Ton Wienbelt*
Photo editor: *TextCase*
Production: *TextCase*
Translation: *Andrew May for First Edition Translations Ltd.*
Typesetting: *M. Gregori for First Edition Translations Ltd.*
Typesetting this edition: *Playne Books Limited*

Photographic credits

Internationaal Bloembollen Centrum, Hillegom: pp. 5 left, 14 left, 16 right, 20 top, 21 top, 27, 32 left, 38 left, 43, 45, 46, 47, 48, 49, 50, 52, 53, 55, 56, 58, 59, 61, 62, 65 top, 66, 69, 75, 76, 78, 80, 81, 82, 83, 84, 85, 87, 89, 92, 93, 94, 95, 98, 99 left, 100, 101, 102 top, 103, 105, 106, 107, 108, 110, 111, 112, 113, 114, 115, 118 right, 127, 132 right
K. Noordhuis, Leens: page 4
Fa. Onderwater, Lisse: pp. 5 right, 6, 7, 8 left and right, 10, 11, 12, 13, 14 right, 18, 19, 20 bottom, 21 bottom, 22, 23, 25, 26 left, 28, 29, 30, 31, 32 right, 38 right, 42, 44, 51, 54, 57, 60, 63, 64, 65 bottom, 68, 70, 71, 72, 73, 74 top, 79, 86, 88, 90, 96, 97, 99 right, 102 bottom, 104, 109, 123, 125, 130 right, 131, 132 left, 133, 135, 136, 137, 141
H. Reitsma, Den Andel: pp. 9, 15, 16 left, 17, 24, 26 right, 33, 34, 35, 36, 37, 38 bottom left, 39, 40, 41, 74 bottom, 77
N. Vermeulen, Groningen: pp. 91, 116, 117, 118 left, 119, 120, 121, 126, 128, 129, 130 left

Contents

Introduction

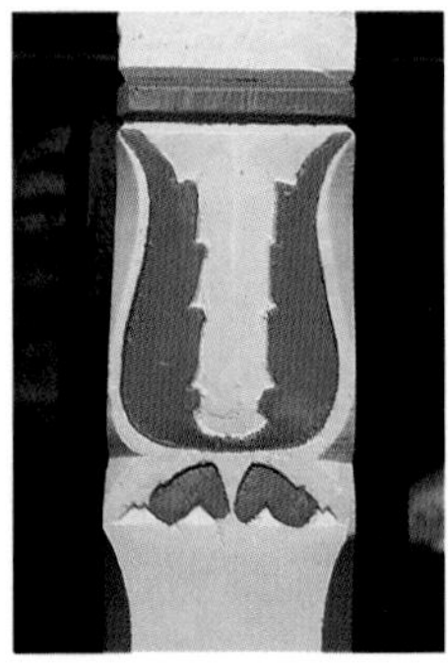

One of my earliest memories from when I was a very young child is of seeing potatoes and onions sprouting in the kitchen refrigerator in the early spring. In a child's way I thought this was the most wonderful and mysterious thing imaginable. Somewhat later, when I grew a sweet potato tuber beside the porch and was rewarded with a luxurious set of rapidly growing vines, I was hooked in a way that every gardener understands. In hindsight, I was lucky to have used a tuber dependable and fast enough in its growth to satisfy a child's short attention span. But regardless of that, and even though I have since become a botanist, horticulturist, landscape designer and teacher, I still feel the amazement I felt as a child at the power of these below-ground chunks to produce such wonderfully different above-ground plants. In bulbs and tubers, corms and rhizomes, the mysterious sense of hidden power, promise, pattern, predictability and increase hold me, as probably many others, in willing thrall.

Many bulbous plants are easily grown and rewarding in their show. Many propagate their underground parts with scarcely any efforts required by the gardener. It is easy for the beginner to become bewildered in deciding what to grow just as easily as it is to be rewarded once begun.

This said, there are still occasions when difficulties are bound to arise. A pest or disease will strike, a location may not be ideal or the plant's hardiness may be uncertain. It is amazing how sometimes the very potential for these problems can turn the process of growing a bulbous plant into a positive challenge. I experienced this when, after several years of attempting–without success–to grow Foxtail Lily (Eremurus spp.) in an area where its hardiness was questionable, I finally succeeded. The plant has been growing there ever since.

In discussing hardiness, many bulbous and tuberous plants grown in the more northerly parts of North America as tender summer or indoor potted winter bulbs are in fact perfectly good all-year garden plants in the southern parts of the United States. As you read this book you will find such plants discussed in the chapters devoted to greenhouse and indoor bulbous and tuberous plants, as well as the chapter on those of summer.

For those of you who are beginners, and even for those who have already tried their luck on a bulbous plant or two, there is much in this book that will guide you, not only in selecting what to try in your part of North America, but also in preparing for the success of what you plant. This includes planting and general care, as well as what to watch for and do when insect or disease problems strike. You will certainly have your stunning successes, as well as a few disappointments, along the way. But you will quickly find that there is an enduring pleasure in the promise and fulfillment of growing bulbs and tubers.

Sam Benvie

Bulbs, Tubers, and Rhizomes

Bulbs and bulb fields – there is nothing more Dutch and thousands of tourists from all over the world head for them. But in spite of that, these plants do not really originate from the Netherlands.

In everyday parlance, for the sake of convenience we speak of "bulbs", even though from a botanical viewpoint this is not strictly correct. This term will be used in this book in the general chapters, but when discussing individual plants, more precise terminology is used as far as possible.

Botanically, a bulb is a compressed part of the stem, the stem base plate. Thick, fleshy, leafy parts, called tunics or scales, are attached to this. They are called tunics or enclosed scales when they go all round the bulb, as is the case with the tulip and the onion, and gaping scales when they do not cover the bulb completely, as is the case with the hyacinth and the lily.

A tuber is a swollen stem or root containing reserve food materials. Examples are the potato, dahlia, and daylily. When the root tuber is a root – for example, the dahlia – it cannot sprout spontaneously as a part of the old stem has to remain on the tuber.

Corms are swollen, underground stems vertically compressed. Like all stems, they have buds (eyes) that can sprout. Examples are gladiolus, crocus, and cyclamen.

Rhizomes are subterranean stem parts, usually growing horizontally with roots and buds. The buds can sprout and form stems above the ground. Examples of this are lily-of-the-valley and wood anemone.

A number of ferns (for example the "hen and chicken fern" from New Zealand) and some alpine plants produce small bulblets, known as offsets. Orchids have tuberous-like organs which cannot be counted

as real bulbs or tubers. These plants therefore have not been taken into consideration in this book.

Even the common snowdrop is still frequently taken from the wild in Turkey. In some areas, they often used to be cultivated in what were known as "snowdrop woods." Snowdrops are perennial bulbs which can be lifted only once every couple of years.

Where do the bulbs come from?

Bulbous and tuberous plants, familiar to most people, occur in the wild mostly in the Mediterranean region, Turkey and the Middle East. In general, those bulbous plants which require more warmth and which are thought of as summer bulbs come from Africa, notably South Africa, as well as California and Mexico. Some bulbous plants come from South America, primarily Peru and Chile.

Bulbs in cultivation

Most of the world's bulbs are cultivated in the Netherlands and a number of species are also cultivated in other countries and then sold in the Netherlands, the world center of the bulb trade. In North America, the primary area of bulb production is the Pacific Northwest.

Less well-known is the sad fact that bulbs such as snowdrops, cyclamen, and urginea are still being taken from the wild. It is preferable to buy these bulbous plants only from companies which can give a reasonable assurance that they are of cultivated origin.

Which bulbs are most important to the nurseryman?

Tulips, narcissi, and hyacinths form the bulk of the cultivated spring bulbous plants, followed by irises and crocuses. Of the summer-flowering plants, the dahlia and gladiolus are the most important. The

Large-scale cultivation of dahlias. Many flowers are used for the floats in flower parades.

other "secondary" plants are cultivated only to a small extent, as they are often not suitable for large-scale cultivation. For the garden, they signify a splendid addition to the range.

The history of cultivation

The plant written about most is the tulip, by far the most important cultivated bulb plant. In Persia, by the twelfth- and thirteenth-century, poets were already singing the praises of the tulip. Around 1560, descriptions of tulips in Turkish gardens appeared. The tulip was first described in Western Europe by Conrad Gesner (after whom the Gesneria plant genus is named). At the time of the reign of Emperor Ferdinand I, the Austrian ambassador to Turkey brought some tulips home with him. Long before this, the Turks had been busy cultivating special tulips and more than a thousand varieties had already been grown and described. In the Low Countries, i.e., the present-day Netherlands and Belgium, the first pictures of tulips appeared in Dodonaeus' *Herbal* (1568). Gradually, the tulip also became popular in the Netherlands, and beginning in 1620 this developed into wild speculation called "tulipomania" or "tulip madness."

With rising prices, more people wanted to be involved in the trade, in which a single bulb (which had not yet even been lifted) was exchanged by contract between various owners. In this way, it was possible for the price of a bulb to rise to over 250 times the annual salary of a laborer by 1636. The crash of February 1637 caused prices to plummet, leaving many families penniless.

At that time, almost 5,000 varieties of tulip were being traded, most of them in very small quantities. Little was learned from history: a century later there was speculation in hyacinth bulbs, though admittedly prices stayed a bit lower. Double-flowered hyacinths were particularly popular.

Still, bulb cultivation continued to spread, especially when, by 1900, the flowers of bulbs had become an important trade commodity.

TIP

Some tubers, such as the winter aconite and the anemone, feel very hard. The uneven small corms are rock hard when they are dry. Prior to being planted out, these plants must be soaked in water for at least half a day.

Nomenclature, the naming of plants

In each country and even in each region, plants used to have a different name. Early on, scholars used Latin names, often describing characteristics of a plant. *Tulipa latifolia alboflore coccineuis lineis ac flammis* vario admittedly gives a clear description, but it also leads to great confusion. In 1753 Carl von Linné (Carolus Linnaeus) introduced a scientific system for all plants.

The plants were classified in descending ranks of class, order, family, genus, species and variety. The introduction of a binary nomenclature was important: every plant has to be described with two names: a generic name and a species name. The first is always written with a capital letter; the second with a small letter. Species are further divided into subspecies and varieties (thus natural variation), which are written with a small letter, and cultured varieties or strains, sometimes denoted by the term "cultivar" (developed by man), which are written with a capital letter. In order to distinguish even more clearly from natural varieties, these names are always placed in single quotes. It can thus be seen directly from the name whether the plant in question originates from nature or whether it has been cultivated in a nursery or a botanical garden and does not occur in nature.

Bulbs are often sold loose in the market. The really special species cannot always be found there.

This information can be useful, for example, if you wish to plant only natural plants in your nature garden. Thus *Muscari aucheri* is a natural species of grape hyacinth from Turkey. Natural species are always printed in italics in this book. *Muscari aucheri* 'Dark Eyes' is a nursery selection with a prettier blue color. This strain will continue by means of vegetative propagation alone, often a human activity.

With many plants, but particularly with bulbs, botanists are not always in agreement with regard to nomenclature. Sometimes a plant is placed in different families by different experts, and different names are often used for one plant genus. When there is scientific agreement on a certain name, many growers seem not to stick to it. In most nursery catalogs, frankly, scant regard is paid to nomenclature. What is remarkable is that precisely those growers who do not come from the world of botany but who cultivate bulbous plants for the enthusiast are the ones who pay such close attention to nomenclature. Often these growers are themselves great enthusiasts for interesting varieties and they appreciate the importance of good nomenclature. The catalogs from these growers are thus very different from the big mail-order company catalogs which are often in splendid color. In this book I have relied on data from the trusty enthusiast nurseryman for nomenclature. There will, however, always be differences of opinion on this subject.

Dahlia *'Bonne Louis'*

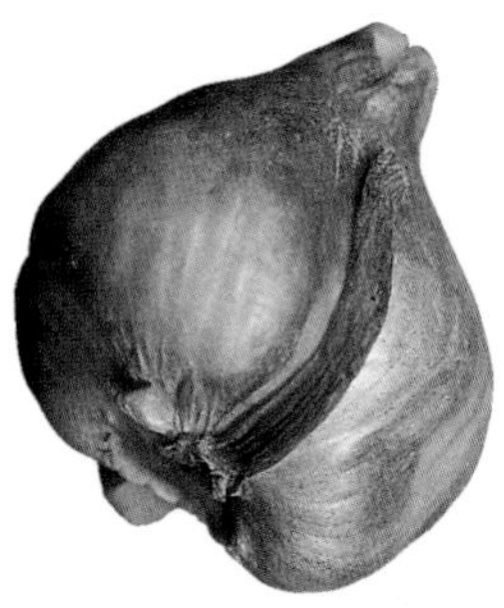

The old flower stem from the previous year can still be seen on this tulip bulb.

Common names

Quite a few bulbous plants have no common name. Often only those plants which are native, or have grown in the country for a long time have one (or several) names. In some plant books an attempt is made to give all bulbous plants a common name, but as long as these names are not generally accepted, this can only increase the chaos with regard to nomenclature.

TIP

When the bulbs of the crown imperial are held in the hand you can actually smell them. After planting, this penetrating smell even goes through to the soil. It is said that moles hate it, but in my garden the moles have come as close as 6ft (2m) to the bulbs. The flowers also have a sickly smell, which can be detected even from a distance.

Bulb Facts: Information on New Varieties, Propagation, Mulching, and Diseases

Like all other plants, bulbous plants need good care to obtain optimum flowering.

Parrot tulip 'Estella Rijnveld': striped and spotted is very much in vogue.

New strains sometimes develop spontaneously, but usually growers have to go to a great deal of trouble to grow a plant with new characteristics. In order to obtain a better crop of plants, it is possible to select and propagate the plant with the prettiest flowers (positive selection) and it is also possible to remove the plants with the worst characteristics (negative selection). These methods are applied in the case of plants from which seed is obtained.

In the case of bulbous plants, certain plants with certain characteristics are often crossed with each other. By means of such hybridization, a particular color, a better resistance to certain diseases, or strong long stems in snowdrops can be achieved. Sometimes colors are in fashion for a certain time: striped tulips, for example, are once again in demand.

Plant breeders' rights

Various international agreements make it possible for plant breeders' rights to be granted on a number of bulbous and tuberous plants. This includes the gladiolus, hyacinth, tulip, iris, lily, narcissus, nerine, and freesia. The rights are granted in order to protect a plant breeder, for he has not stinted on cost or trouble in order to develop a new cultivar.

Plant breeders' rights give the sole right to cultivate, market or hold in stock (cultivated) plants from a (new) cultivar. Plant breeders' rights on a specific plant are valid for varying number of years depending on the country in which the rights are registered. A registered, and thus protected cultivar, is often marked ®. Many bulbs are grown under licence. This means that a sort of royalty (fee) has to be paid to the plant breeder title holder, usually the person who developed the strain. This is why new strains are often more expensive than the strains which have already been on the market for ten years.

TIP

Natural plant species can easily be crossed. This mixing rarely occurs in the wild due to the fact that as a rule the different species do not grow close to one another. In gardens, many plants are placed next to one another, so the species can then cross. It is rarer for different plant genera to cross. This occurs only when both plants come from the same family. It is customary to place the letter x before the name of these bigeneric hybrids (genus hybrids). Here are some examples:
x *Amarcrinum* (syn. *Crinodonna*) (*Amaryllis* x *Crinum*)
x *Amarygia* (*Amaryllis* x *Brunsvigia*)
x *Gladanthera* (*Gladiolus* x *Acidanthera*)

Sizes

The codes DN I, DN II, and DN III are used in the case of narcissi to indicate the quality of the bulbs. Many other plants are sized using I (largest size) to III (smallest size).
In the case of other bulbs, the circumference of the bulb in centimeters is used as a starting point. This is difficult for the layman, as he does not know the average bulb circumference of a specific plant in either imperial or metric measure.
Narcissi are sold by the piece and also often by the pound (kilogram). In order to find out the quantity of bulbs, the buyer needs to know how many bulbs there are of any size in a pound (kilogram).
When trading between themselves, growers also deal in beds of bulbs which have not yet been lifted.

Packaging

Special offers of 100 or 250 bulbs prettily gift-wrapped often seem to be very good value, but when bulbs are packaged in this way, you should pay attention to the contents: nearly always there are only a few of the more desirable sorts of bulbs. The cartons are often "filled up" with the cheaper grape hyacinth, allium, and botanical crocus.
The sizes of the packed bulbous plants should be shown on the packaging. It often looks as though only the smaller sizes have been packed: only the packaging can be seen and not the bulbs! When buying dahlias, look beyond the picture on the packaging to compare the size of the tubers in the packet, as there can be great differences.
As a rule, the cost of the high-quality packaging is at the expense of bulb quality. In the final analysis, it is the flowering bulbs which matter and not the colorful packaging. These packets are often kept in shops which are too warm, greatly reducing the quality of the bulbs, particularly late in the buying season.
Many types of bulbs can still be bought loose from specialized sales companies so you can buy by the piece, and the bulb size can be seen clearly.

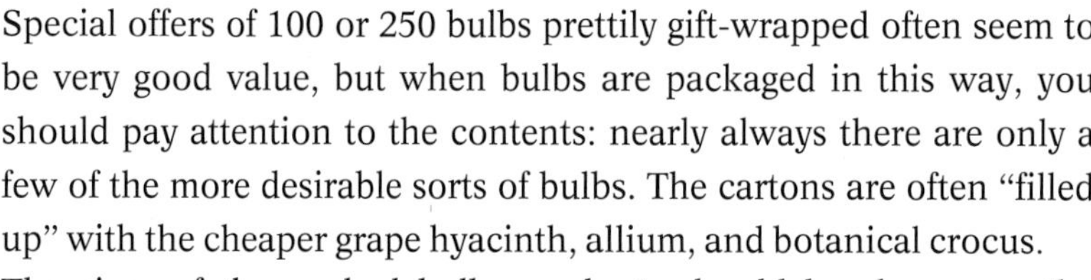

Bulbs being sorted by machine.

Species which propagate themselves

Self-generative propagation occurs in few bulbous and tuberous plants. Small-flowered crocuses propagate themselves well. You can also give this propagation a helping hand. When the crocuses have almost died back, the seed capsules can be seen just above the ground. Gather them and sow the seed straight away in other spots in the garden. In two or three years you will have more flowering corms. Snowdrops and winter aconites also propagate themselves in some places depending on environmental circumstances.

Winter aconites sometimes seem to prefer lime-rich sites with a lot of stones or gravel in the soil: some gravel paths become totally covered with this plant. The quamash propagates itself in damp places. Puschkinia spreads well on clay soil. *Anemone nemorosa* seems to spread quickly, but in its case, the rhizomes spread out underground, especially where the soil has a high organic content. The holewort or hollow root, *Corydalis cava*, can also be sown. Keep the seed from the white blooms separate from the purple ones in order to make color combinations. They can be sown in pots, to be planted out later. For all bulbous plants, seed should be sown as soon as it is ripe on the plant. This is particularly the case with the cyclamen, the seed of which can dry out very quickly.

Bulbs are often sold loose in the market. The really special kinds cannot always be found there.

Propagating bulbs yourself

Let us start with the simplest: snowdrops. Once every three years, the clumps of snowdrops can be lifted and divided by hand into three, four, or more parts. This job is best done when the snowdrops are growing or flowering.

Take care that the roots are not damaged too much. No lateral roots grow on the roots of bulbous plants. Water is taken up solely by the end of the root and for this reason it must not be broken.

After a few years, you will have a garden full of snowdrops, and what is more, they will grow better as they are once again in fresh soil which is not exhausted.

The corms of some tuberous plants, such as the winter aconite and the anemone, feel very hard. The uneven small corms are rock hard when dry. Prior to being planted out these corms must be soaked in water for at least half a day.

In some places, snowdrops propagate themselves. You can give the plants in these spots a helping hand and spread them over the garden yourself. The bluebell and meadow saffron can also be divided and planted out during the growing season – the spring – which will produce great quantities after a few years. You can be sure that when you see gardens where these plants are everywhere, an enthusiast has been busy dividing the plants.

Propagation does not happen on its own. The only plants which spread themselves over large distances are *Crocus tomasinianus*, a botanical crocus, and *Allium ursinum*, the wild or bear's garlic.

The hyacinth is quite another story. Before planting, cut a star or a small hollow in the base of the bulb using a sharp kitchen knife. New bulblets will form on the cuts and will flower after three years. The young bulblets must be collected from the parent bulb and planted out after one year.

The flowers of this Muscari armeniacum *'Blue Spike' are pretty, but the foliage is badly wilted*

TIP

If you think that your garden is a hopeless case due to wetness, take heart from the list below. Wet ground which stinks when it is dug due to lack of oxygen is fatal for all plants. It needs draining, a good digging, and the addition of humus. The plants listed below like permanent wetness, at any rate moisture-retentive ground:

Camassia cusickii
Camassia esculenta
Camassia leichtlinii
Fritillaria meleagris
Leucojum aestivum
Leucojum vernum

Soil type and mulching

It is not only the soil type, but primarily the dampness of the soil which is important. Do not merely cover tender plants, but also put them in drier ground to prevent damage. Some plants, such as camassia and fritillaries, are perfectly happy in damp or wet ground. Most other bulbous plants prefer clay soil. There is still satisfactory choice for people who live in sandy soil areas too, but the bulbous plants will spread less quickly. The following are best suited to sandy soil: *Allium* species, wood anemone, *Corydalis solida, Eremurus*, gladiolus, and *Crocus tomasinianus* and, with good mulching, dahlias.

With regard to mulching, consideration must be given to the growing cycle of the bulbs. It is the opposite way round compared to the other garden plants. There is not much sense in mulching bulbs when the shrubs and permanent plants need to be mulched: the bulbs are, after all, still dormant.

Sprinkle slow-acting organic dressings in the fall, so that the bulbs can benefit from them during their root-growing period in the winter, or fast-acting fertilizer in the early spring, immediately after the last frost. This dressing will then be used for foliage growth after flowering, so that stronger bulbs are formed for the following season.

When planting bulbs on poor sandy ground, mix compost with the soil; on heavy clay soil, garden peat should be used. Peaty soil is rich enough in humus already.

Diseases and pests

Most plants, whether they be roses, fruit trees or annuals, are prey to a host of diseases and pests, but with bulbous and tuberous plants we can happily be brief about these depressing matters.

As a rule, small bulbous plants are not often troubled by disease. During their early flowering season, lice or snails are not yet active. It is true that squirrels, chipmunks, and the like can cause great damage.

Field voles make use of mole tunnels, so eradicating moles is an indirect way of protecting your bulbs. Field voles should not be confused with the useful insect-eating shrews, which should be left in peace. In addition to getting rid of moles, keeping the grass short is a good method of control. Grassy verges and slopes in particular offer good living conditions for field voles.

Do not plant tulips in the same site where they were planted in the previous year. If that cannot be avoided, for example in a limited space, disinfect the ground with a suitable disinfectant. The *Rhizoctonia* mold attacks the bulbs before a second season's flowering. As with the rose nematode in a site with roses, this ground mold can be suppressed by planting the bed with African marigolds in the summer. Dig in all the African marigold plants in the fall before the new bulbs go into the ground. Chop the marigolds finely first, using a very sharp spade.

Professional growers use Rhizolex as a chemical control against this mold but it is not available in small quantities.

Narcissi can be affected by the larvae of the narcissus fly (*Merodon equestris*). Like its flesh-colored larvae, the lily beetle (*Lilioceris lilii*), a small beetle which can easily be recognized by its black and orange coloring, attacks the leaves of the lily and the fritillary. A relation of the leaf beetle, *Lilioceris merdigera*, is more orange than black. It feeds on other plants of the lily family: lily-of-the-valley and Solomon's seal. The best method of control is to catch and remove the beetles by hand.

Puschkinia scilloides *var.* libanotica *propagates itself well here on moderately heavy clay ground. The young shoots will flower in two years' time.*

Dividing must be done by hand; the bulbs should also be halved using a spade.

Clumps of snowdrops or harebells can easily be divided when they are in full leaf. Take care not to damage the roots.

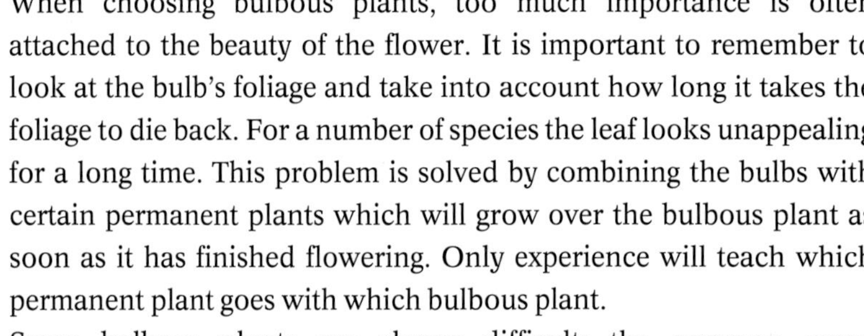

Foliage dying back

When choosing bulbous plants, too much importance is often attached to the beauty of the flower. It is important to remember to look at the bulb's foliage and take into account how long it takes the foliage to die back. For a number of species the leaf looks unappealing for a long time. This problem is solved by combining the bulbs with certain permanent plants which will grow over the bulbous plant as soon as it has finished flowering. Only experience will teach which permanent plant goes with which bulbous plant.

Some bulbous plants are always difficult: the common grape hyacinth, for example, always has a great quantity of foliage. It is a pity that on the packaging mention is made only of the flower color, height and flowering period, and not of the much longer time that a bulbous plant looks ugly. For this reason, plant only the earliest flowering plants in the lawn. The dying foliage can be cut off when the leaves are turning yellow; it is not necessary to wait until the foliage is totally withered.

TIP

In view of the places where most bulbous plants come from (the Mediterranean area, the Middle East, Turkey, and South Africa), it is not surprising that not all bulbous plants are hardy in cold climates. Some can actually remain in the ground provided that they are covered with straw or garden peat. With tender plants it is a good idea to cover them with a plate of glass or some plastic: dry peat insulates better than wet peat. For this reason, do not plant the following plants in ground which is too moist:

Anemone coronaria
Crocosmia
Eremurus
***Gladiolus* (small-flowered)**
Hyacinthus
Ipheion
***Iris* (hollandica varieties)**
Ixia
Liatris spicata
Oxalis adenophylla

Planting and After-Care

When and how deep should bulbs be planted in the ground? How many bulbs can be planted close to each other? These are burning questions, especially for the beginning gardener.

Hyacinthoides hispanica, *the bluebell, as mass planting. The advantage of this is that bluebells do not have to be lifted. When the foliage has died back, a variegated ivy again comes into view.*

Planting depth The general rule is to plant the bulb twice as deep as the bulb is wide. Of course, there are exceptions: snowdrops, for example, must be planted somewhat deeper in dry ground. Under trees, the top layer of the ground can certainly dry out greatly in the summer. In moisture-retentive ground the rule holds good. It is not necessary to go into the garden with a ruler: the bulb has its own mechanism to fix its own depth. Using pushing or pulling roots, the bulb can pull itself deeper into the ground or push itself up correctly, depending on what it prefers. After a few years, the permanent plants in this way will have determined their own depth.

The following measurements give a rough guideline for the following plants:

anemone	1 in	(2 cm)
ranunculus	1¼ in	(3 cm)
bluebell	1½ in	(4 cm)
crocus (botanical)	2 in	(5 cm)
grape hyacinth	2½ in	(6 cm)
snowdrop	2½–4 in	(6-10 cm)
crocus (large-flowered)	2½ in	(6 cm)
tuberous begonia	2½ in	(6 cm)
crown imperial	4–6 in	(10-15 cm)
tulip	3–6 in	(7.5-15 cm)

Crocus *'Pickwick'*.

glory of the snow	3–4 in	(7.5-10 cm)
narcissus	3–6 in	(7.5-15 cm)
gladiolus	4–6 in	(10-15 cm)
lily (except *Lilium candidum)*	4–6 in	(10-15 cm)
dahlia	5–6 in	(12.5-15 cm)
hyacinth	6–7 in	(15-18 cm)

Anemone coronaria *mixed and single-colored.*

It is not only planting depth which is important – spacing must also be given consideration. As a rule of thumb, I plant ten small spring bulbs in an area the size of a saucer.

A number of species can be planted in small clusters; others can be scattered, and after a number of years they will create their own clusters. Bulbs are not attractive when they are planted in rows: in order to keep more or less the same spacing, scatter the bulbs on the ground first and then plant them individually.

Planting baskets

So you can find the bulbs again, use plastic planting baskets. These baskets, which are 10 in (25 cm) in diameter and 4 in (10 cm) high, have openings on all sides so root growth is not stunted. When annuals are to be planted on the site of the bulbous plants after flowering, the bulb baskets can be pulled out of the ground and they and the bulbs moved elsewhere. If you want to produce a garden which is always in flower, you can replace the baskets in the border with baskets which are filled with later-flowering bulbous plants. This is a labor-intensive task, but one which gives a great deal of satisfaction.

Care during growth and flowering

In bulb cultivation, straw is often used to cover the flower bulbs, but in a home garden this is not very attractive. Garden peat is a better solution in this case. The greatest disadvantage of garden peat is that it blows away in the wind. Keep fallen leaves to use as covering material. A piece of wire netting over the top will stop them from blowing away.

Protection

Christmas tree branches also provide good protection, although a period of frost can, of course, occur before Christmas. Ask at your garden center whether any trees are left over from the Christmas sale: they will be grateful to you for saving them the removal costs.

Remove the material immediately after the last frost, roughly half-way through March. This of course must be done earlier in the case of some plants which flower in February, and in areas where spring arrives early.

Tying up

Spring bulbs do not need to be tied up to prevent them from being blown down. Only some tall fritillaries and species of allium are inclined to fall down. Plant the bulbs deeply enough, so that the plants are not blown away, bulb and all. Summer-flowering bulbs such as Dutch irises, tall dahlias, lilies, and gladioli frequently need to be supported.

The plants are suitable in the separate patch for cut flowers, as the unattractive supporting material must always be put up early in the season. Bean canes can be used for support. Plastic rings can be purchased at garden centers. These rings can be raised while the plant is growing.

Many people want a garden which does not require much maintenance. One criterion for this is that no bulbs must be used which have to be lifted annually. A second criterion is that the plants must not need to be staked in order to prevent them from being blown down. The following plants are therefore not suitable: Dahlia (tall varieties)
Gladiolus (the large-flowered ones)
Iris (hollandica varieties)
Lilium.

Crop rotation

Most bulbous plants can remain on the same site for years on end, especially the naturalizing bulbs. It is different with tulips, hyacinths, and irises. The chance of infection with viruses and bacteria increases with each year. For this reason, do not plant these bulbs on the same sites over a long period unless you treat the plant holes with specific pesticides each year. To me this method now seems out-of-date for garden use.
For cut-flower production, crop rotation is much better for these plants. Make a cultivation plan for the cut-flower section, in the same way as for the vegetable patch. This will keep the risks of *Botrytus* (fire), *Sclerotium* (gray bulb rot), and *Fusarium* (basal rot) to a minimum. Annual cut flowers can be sown or planted the following year on the site where the bulbous plants were.

Seed capsules

Professional growers cut back tulips when they are only just in flower. They do this so that the energy which would otherwise go toward forming fruit goes to the bulb. Of course, in gardens this is not done just as the flowers are going to blossom, but when the petals start to fall off. Tulips and narcissi in particular should be cut back. In the case of narcissi, it is neater when they are cut back, as the flowers dry up and the petals do not fall off. Just pull the narcissus seed capsules off by hand; with tulips, simply break the stalk.

The seed capsules of the *Fritillaria imperialis* (crown imperial), *Lilium martagon* (common Turk's-cap lily), and many other plants are part of the ornamental value of these plants. On no account remove them! The crown imperial even owes its name to the crown of seed capsules which stand up in a ring when ripening. This same phenomenon can be seen in the Turk's-cap lily.

TIP

Some tuberous plants can climb. Only a few tuberous plants have stems which form tendrils. They die back to the ground again each year. The white bryony is poisonous. The tuberous rhizome of the lathyrus is edible. The following are climbers:

***Aconitum volubile* – climbing monkshood**

Dichelostemma volubile

***Bryonia cretica* ssp. *dioica* – white bryony**

***Gloriosa rothschildiana* – climbing lily**

***Lathyrus tuberosus* - Perennial Sweet Pea**

When to lift

Spring bulbs which have to be lifted, as well as tulips and hyacinths, can be removed from the ground when the foliage has died back fully. Insert short canes between the bulbs, soon after they have died back, as otherwise you will not be able to find the bulbs. Summer bulbs such as dahlias, begonias, and gladioli are lifted at the end of October or beginning of November. This could be immediately after the first night frost. Although the foliage may be frozen, the frost has not yet penetrated into the ground.

Storing bulbs

Bulbs that can remain in the ground are the simplest. When planting, remember to insert a short stick, otherwise you will soon forget where the bulbs were planted. Tulips and hyacinths can be lifted better once the foliage has died back. Keep these bulbs fairly warm, above 70°F (20°C) during the summer. The quality of hyacinths will decline despite being stored well and after two years it is better just to buy fresh bulbs again.

Professional growers store bulbs in gauze trays. These are cases whose bases are made of gauze so that ventilation between the bulbs is improved. Dahlias and gladioli can be stored in dry garden peat, but some people prefer sharp sand. Using the latter material, the chance of rotting is smaller, but the chance of drying out is greater. Dahlias in particular will shrivel up if they are too dry. If they have not dried out, but are very shriveled, they can easily be planted again. They will grow again as usual, but with a bit more difficulty. Farmers used to store dahlias in the stable above the horses: frost-free and in the correct humidity.

A grower's cooling chamber. The bulbs here are kept at the correct temperature and are well-ventilated.

Prepared bulbs

Bulbs are often specially prepared for indoor flowering. A special temperature treatment ensures that the bulbs will flower in December or January in the warm environment of the room. The grower has already provided the cold spell the bulb needs in order to flower and the bulbs will be brought into flower immediately in the warmth of the house. Afterwards, these forced bulbs are of little value, though it is of course still worth taking the trouble to plant them out in the garden.

Where to buy bulbous plants

Traditionally bulbs are dispatched by specialist mail-order houses, because in contrast to other plants they are easy to send during their dormant period. Most garden centers sell bulbs, and many florists and department stores carry them too. Packed bulbs have become an ordinary supermarket commodity, but remember that bulbs in heated stores are not in the best storage place: the quality of many plants quickly deteriorates.

The greatest choice is generally to be found at the garden center, where the garden peat which is needed to cover the bulbs after planting can be bought at the same time as the bulbs. The choice, especially of less common bulbs, is even greater with some specialized mail-order firms. Some growers apply themselves to growing specialty bulbous plants and frequently also produce catalogs. Their addresses can usually be found in magazines for plant enthusiasts.

Bulbs are selected by hand on a conveyor belt: diseased and damaged bulbs are removed.

Mixed or single-colored

For a number of plants, the bulbs are supplied almost entirely mixed, especially with summer bulbs. A packet with a picture of different colors all intermixed looks very cheerful. It is easy to forget that when they are planted out in the garden, all sorts of other different flowers with different colors will also be mixed in with them and the flowers will be less striking.

Another disadvantage of mixed plants is that not all strains of a

From the greigii *group:* Tulipa *'Plaisir'.*

particular species are equally tall: *Anemone blanda* 'White Splendour', for example, will outgrow the blue and pink members of its species.

Left: In this market stall, bulbs are sold both loose and pre-packed.

Right: Fritillaria *bulbs are lifted in the field.*

Naturalized Gardens

Some gardeners want to have only naturalizing plants in their garden. There are naturalizing plants among the bulbous plants too: plants which were deliberately planted out and then became naturalized.

A hybrid product of Hyacinthoides hispanica *and* H. non-scripta. *This plant can often be seen in old stone ruin settings.*

In country estates and in gardens near old homesteads, in graveyards and near old farmhouses, plants can often be found *en masse* which hardly occur elsewhere in the surrounding region. By naturalized plants we mean plants whose distribution is restricted to specific areas, usually around old stone houses, country estates, old farms and similar environments such as churchyards and dry stone walls. As a rule, they frequently consist of species and varieties with striking blooms which had previously been deliberately introduced and which then became naturalized and indigenous to that area.

Origins of naturalizing bulbs

Many spring bulbs come from the Mediterranean region and from Asia Minor. They were introduced here over the past century and a half by the well-to-do and, of course, by botanists. Other plants come from Europe or are indigenous to certain places within North America. These plants were often introduced to country estates, for example, and knew how to hold their ground there without receiving any care to speak of.

Bulbs as naturalizing plants

A number of shrubs (for example, forsythia), permanent plants (for example, bugleweed and the small periwinkle), and bulbs are considered to be naturalizing plants. Many come from the Mediterranean or from mountainous regions. The dates when they were first introduced are not entirely clear, but the year in which the specific plant was first described is known. The dates written after the plants indicate this.

The abbreviations refer to the country where this plant was first described (E = England, Swt = Switzerland, G = Germany, N = the Netherlands).

***Allium ursinum* (N 1561)**
wild garlic
bear's garlic, ramsons, wood garlic

A. vineale
crow garlic
false garlic, stag's garlic

***Anemone blanda* (E 1898)**
windflower

***A. nemorosa* (Swt 1883)**
wood anemone

Naturalized plants feel at home in this environment. The riverbanks here are totally covered with wild garlic, Allium ursinum.

Ornithogalum umbellatum.

***Arum italicum* (E 1683)**	Italian arum lily Lords and Ladies
***A. maculatum* (Middle Ages)**	variegated arum lily common cuckoo pint, Variegated Lords and Ladies
Chionodoxa sardensis	glory of the snow A plant which was introduced only this century
***Colchicum byzantinum* (Swt 1561)**	meadow saffron
***Convallaria majalis* (N 1420)**	lily-of-the-valley

Left: Eranthis hyemalis.

Right: In this naturalized area Allium ursinum *(wild or bear's garlic) can be seen in the foreground.*

***Corydalis cava* (E1596)**	holewort, hollow root
***C. solida* (E 1596)**	fumewort bird on a bush, bird in a thorn
***Crocus tomasinianus* (E1847)**	
***C. vernus* (N 1550)**	spring crocus
***Eranthis hyemalis* (B 1570)**	winter aconite
***Erythronium dens-canis* (N1594)**	dog's-tooth violet, trout lily

***Fritillaria meleagris* (N1572)**	snake's-head fritillary, chequered lily
Gagea lutea	yellow star of Bethlehem
Galanthus elwesii	snowdrop
G. ikariae	
***G. nivalis* (Middle Ages)**	
***G. nivalis* 'Plenus'**	
***Hyacinthoides bifolia* (N1594)**	
H. non-scripta	English bluebell
***Leucojum aestivum* (N1594)**	summer snowflake

A fine plant for a smallish pot: Iris reticulata, *the 'Harmony' variety of which has the prettiest blue flowers.*

Corydalis bulbosa. *The purple-pink and the white plants are usually mixed*

L. vernum (long cultivated)	spring snowflake
***Lilium martagon* (Swt 1830)**	Turk's-cap lily
Muscari armeniacum	grape hyacinth
***Narcissus poeticus* 'Actaea'**	the poet's narcissus, pheasant's eye daffodil
N. pseudonarcissus* ssp *major	wild daffodil, trumpet narcissus, yellow narcissus
***Ornithogalum umbellatum* (N1594)**	star of Bethlehem

***Saxifraga granulata* 'Plena'** meadow saxifrage

***Scilla sibirica* (E 1796)** Siberian squill, spring squill

***S. tubergeniana* (N1931)**

***Tulipa sylvestris* (N1594)** wild tulip

Local plant names

Some plants have no common names; others have different names in different areas. There are plants which are known by many names, and different plants can be known by the same name. The many common names for naturalizing plants make it crystal clear that these plants have been grown for a long time.

In some countries, names have been standardized only in this century, 250 years after the Swedish botanist Linnaeus introduced individual scientific names for all plants. Apart from a few changes, this naming system, known as "binominal nomenclature," is still in use.

TIP

The following bulbs grow well even in permanent deep shade, for example on the north side of the house. As the spring-flowering bulbous plants come into leaf early, there are many more species which grow well under trees. About half-way through May, when the trees come into leaf and the ground is in shade, the bulbs are once again at the end of their growing cycle. Whereas all permanent plants shy away from such a site as it becomes too dry under the old trees in summer, bulbous plants offer numerous possibilities, for example:

Allium ursinum
Arum italicum
A. maculatum
Convallaria majalis
Corydalis cava
C. solida
Lilium martagon

The Various Uses of Flowering Bulbs

Should bulbs be lifted each year or left in the ground? A number of bulbs have to be lifted annually; others can usually be left in the ground.

Allium sphaerocephalum *can be planted in groups in the border, but it can also be planted individually and spread throughout the whole border.*

Cultivated tulips and hyacinths should be lifted when the foliage has died back. The other spring-flowering bulbs stay in the ground and most species, on the right site, will spread when left to themselves. Cyclamens actually have to stay put for years to flower abundantly.
In contrast, the summer-flowering bulbs all have to be lifted in the fall to overwinter inside except in frost-free areas. Most are not hardy; others can tolerate cold but not wet conditions. If you do not intend to pay much attention to your bulbs later on, then get only spring bulbs which naturalize well and which can thus also spread themselves.

For the border

Grass in which bulbs are planted cannot be mown for quite some time. If you are one of the many people who dislike the untidy appearance of the out-of-flower bulbs and the long grass, plant your bulbs in your perennial plant border. Choose the early-flowering species for this: the perennial plants grow more quickly in the spring than you think. The less attractive foliage of the bulbs will quickly disappear from view. Summer plants which grow taller can also be "intertwined" among the permanent plants.

For the rock garden

The rock garden is a refined part of the garden. Many species are displayed to their best advantage in small quantities here. In a medium-sized garden, a small bag of flowering bulbs, which usually does not contain more than fifteen bulbs, will practically be lost, but in the rock garden, there is no need for any larger quantity. Keep each species separate and plant at least ten of the small bulblets in an area the size of a saucer. To bring variety to the rock garden, choose many different species. In the final analysis, a rock garden imitates natural conditions.

For flower beds

A number of plants, such as tulips, hyacinths, and most summer-flowering bulbs, have to be lifted each year. For this reason, plant these bulbs only where rummaging around in the soil does not present a problem. Thus large-flowered tulips in the heather garden are extremely impractical, to say nothing of the bad combination they make.

Special flower beds for annuals were very much in fashion in the last century: in winter and early spring, bulbs were combined with biennials such as pansies, double daisies or forget-me-nots, and with a traditional bedding plant such as salvia and African marigolds in the summer. The crown imperial is well suited to flower beds as it has to be planted so deep in the soil that the bedding plants can be planted above the bulbs.

TIP

Bulbous plants in the darkest colors combine most strikingly with bright yellow: each color will intensify the other. In large expanses of color, *Tulipa* 'Queen of Night' forms a combination which has now become practically a tradition with the yellow *Tulipa* 'Golden Apeldoorn'. When making combinations, pay close attention to the flowering periods.

The green areas between the bulbs and shrubs in the background lend some tranquility to this bright mixture of colors.

In grass

A number of bulbous plants lend themselves to use in a lawn. A distinction must be made here between a neatly-mown lawn and grass in an orchard, for example. Orchard grass is mown much later and therefore offers more opportunities for planting a number of late-flowering bulbous plants.

Only the early-flowering bulbs can be planted in the lawn. The easiest are those plants which are inclined toward self-propagation. Do not plant all species mixed up together, but plan in advance which expanses of color should come where. Large-flowered crocus and fall crocus come in a range of colors: lay the colors out separately and where the different colors meet swap a few bulbs around, so that there is a gradual transition from one color to the next. For example, plant a dark color close to a tree trunk and let this gradually change into a light color farther away from the tree. Crocus (of various species and varieties), winter aconite, and Siberian squill are best suited for a grassy site.

Not much work and still an eye-catching result. With a thousand ten-a-penny bulbs, you have a sea of flowers with this Chionodoxa luciliae.

There are more possibilities for bulbs in long grass, as the grass is unlikely to be mown before June. Plants such as the wild tulip and the bluebell and other earlier-flowering plants can be planted here.

If the grass is on moist ground, various fritillaries and quamash plants can also be considered. The white-flowered and fragrant poet's narcissus can be used in larger orchards. In order to be able to enjoy the flowering plants more, mow a "pathway" using a lawn mower, so that the tall grass is not trodden down and you can walk in the area without having to put on your boots or getting wet feet.

TIP

For people who really love collecting dark-colored bulbs in the garden I suggest *Fritillaria zagrica*, *F. armena*, *F. straussii*, *F. tuntasia*, *F. drenovskii* and *F. ehrhartii*. The most stunning of all is *Iris susiana*, the mourning iris. This iris was grown more widely up until twenty years ago. It has now been rediscovered in a small nursery in Israel.

Combinations

Bulbous plants have only a short flowering period. Combinations of different species extend flowering; not just combinations of different types of bulbous plants, but also combinations with permanent plants or shrubs. When planning combinations with shrubs, pay particular attention to proportion. A dwarf shrub next to a tall narcissus is not a pretty sight, nor is it attractive when a tall shrub is still young. But the shrub will grow and with it the correct proportions will automatically be achieved. Grape hyacinths standing on their own have the disadvantage that you have to look at the unattractive foliage for a long time. Combine them with a late-appearing perennial plant, so that the foliage "grows away" between the foliage of this permanent plant. Permanent plants which come into leaf very early are not suitable, as there is the chance that the bulb flowers will be lost in the leaves of the permanent plants.

Bulbs as cut flowers

When planting bulbs, we often think how good they would look as cut flowers, but once they are in flower, we find it a pity to pick them. It is better to grow the plants suitable for cutting in rows in the cut-flower patch: long-stemmed narcissi, crown imperial, tall tulips and summer-flowering dahlias, gladioli and Dutch irises. Support is needed for the summer plants. Put small poles on both sides of the

bed and spread plant netting between them. The netting can be raised up as the plants grow.

In a mixed garden where many large and small bulbous plants are next to each other, every year it is a surprise to see which have seeded and propagated themselves.

Method

In fall, dig in horse manure in an oblong bed 24 to 32 in (60 to 80 cm) wide. Let the bed rest during the winter. In the spring the lumps can be raked over and the netting can be laid on the bed. Put the poles on the outer edge through the mesh of the net. The bulbs can be planted between the mesh on the bed. When the plants begin to grow, the netting is gradually raised up, depending on the height of the plant. At the end of the growing season the netting, which can be bought made of galvanized wire or nylon, can be stored for the following season.

Bulbs as plants for bees

Bees begin to fly in the spring when the temperature is warm enough. By then, snowdrops have often finished flowering, but the crocus, next in bloom, is a good plant for bees, as are the ornamental onion, glory of the snow, hyacinth, harebell, grape hyacinth, and puschkinia, and members of the lily family as a rule. Before the middle of the summer you can oblige the bees with the lathyrus. For late summer, the single-flowered dahlia is of most interest to bees. In June, clivia can also be put outside (in shade). There the flowers will be pollinated and a year later the plant will form splendid red berries. You can propagate the plant very simply from the seed of the berry. Allow only one seed per pot, because in a short time each one will provide a sizeable plant! Take them inside again if you live in a frost-prone area.

Bulbs in containers

First of all: buy only the largest bulb sizes for containers. You can plant the smaller sizes successfully in the garden, where they will also continue to give pleasure in the years to come. But when bulbs are in window boxes for only one year, they must look robust and healthy. By no means all bulbous plants are suitable for containers. The short tulips, short narcissi and hyacinths are suitable, as are all crocuses. A combination with long-flowering pansies is desirable. The smaller species such as chionodoxa, scilla, and puschkinia combine well with rock plants in troughs or tubs. Grape hyacinths have too much foliage and are therefore not suitable for containers. Tulips from the *fosteriana, greigii* and *kaufmanniana* groups have large flowers and short, sturdy stems. Before flowering, these relatively early tulips display attractive foliage. These are the tulips best suited for containers and small flower beds or borders. Leave the containers outside in the winter, but to obtain earlier flowering, put them in a slightly heated garage or greenhouse in February. Flower pots with bulbs in can be heeled into the ground in the fall after planting. Put them on the patio even in the early spring. Pots can also be brought inside whenever there is frost, though if only a night frost is forecast

Grape hyacinth with tulips in a spring garden.

A display garden in its full glory.

they can just as well stay outside. The following varieties of tulip can be considered for flower containers:

***Tulipa fosteriana* group**

'Candela'	yellow
'Mme Lefèbre'	bright red
'Princeps'	red
'Sweetheart'	golden yellow with creamy white
'White Emperor' ('Purissima')	white

***Tulipa greigii* group**

'Calypso'	salmon pink, yellow edged, striped leaf
'Cape Cod'	apricot with yellow
'Corsage'	pink with yellow
'Dreamboat'	yellow, red glow
'King's Orb'	bright red, yellow edged, striped leaf
'Oriental Beauty'	fiery red
'Oriental Splendour'	red with yellow
'Plaisir'	red with yellow
'Red Riding Hood'	bright scarlet
'Sparkling Fire'	vermilion red, striped leaf
'Sweet Lady'	soft pink, purple striped leaf
'Zampa'	soft yellow with bronze

Crocosmias are also often found in bouquets.

Tulipa kaufmanniana group

'Concerto'	creamy yellow, darker center
'Heart's Delight'	crimson red, pale pink edge, striped leaf
'Jeantine'	crimson red with apricot pink
'Johann Strauss'	red, white edge, white inside, striped leaf
'Love Song'	orange-red with yellow
'Shakespeare'	orange-salmon-apricot
'Showwinner'	deep red, yellow center, striped leaf
'Stresa'	red with yellow
'The First'	white with crimson red

Bulbous plants can often be bought already flowering in pots. You pay a lot more for them than if you took the trouble yourself to plant the bulblets and grow them on in the cool in the fall. The ready-prepared pots are good for the window ledge, but can also be transferred to a flower bowl. When the bulbs have finished flowering they can again be planted out in the garden. They may have suffered from such treatment, with the result that they might need one more year to really take hold.

It should be pointed out that flower containers are often on the small side. Therefore fill the containers and bowls up to the top with soil. Not only does this look prettier, but the plants will also grow better in the container with a greater volume of soil. If so desired, there can be a small pouring rim. It goes without saying that there must always be a drainage hole at the bottom of the bowl or container.

Bulbs for naturalization

All bulbous plants which are good self-propagators can be planted out for naturalization. You can choose from the group of naturalizing plants. Plants do not naturalize equally well on all types of soil: to be sure of success, see which bulbous plants occur *en masse* in your neighborhood.

Narcissus, crocus, and grape hyacinth will naturalize in all conditions. Sometime the snowdrop propagates itself, but this depends on the conditions. *Camassia leichtlinii* 'Alba' is the latest-flowering spring bulb which propagates by seed quickly on a reasonably moist site. *Cyclamen hederifolia* propagates easily, especially on heavy clay soil. If you propagate the plants yourself, use only fresh, ripe seed. On no account let the seed dry out. The choice of plants for naturalization also depends on the humus content of the soil and on the moisture. Wood anemones grow well only if there is a thick humus layer into which they can put down the fine small rootstocks more easily than in heavy clay ground.

Although tulips cannot be counted really as naturalizing bulbs, the lily-flowered tulip 'Aladdin', freely scattered from a mixed packet of flowering bulbs, seems to have held its ground in my garden to this day (after ten years).

TIP

In summer there are enough flowers in the garden to be put in a vase. In the spring, it is a different matter. The earliest-flowering plants always have short flower stems. From the beginning of April plants suitable for cutting are in bloom. An exception to this is perhaps the large-flowered snowdrop, *Galanthus elwesii*, which flowers a fortnight earlier than *Galanthus nivalis*. The following species are good for cutting.

Allium giganteum
Allium neapolitanum
Allium sphaerocephalum
Muscari armeniacum
Narcissus
Ornithogalum
Tulipa

Colchicum autumnale is indigenous to deciduous woodlands of west-central Europe.

Bulbs between ground-cover plants

Many bulbs which are suitable for naturalization should be considered for planting between low-lying ground-cover plants. Ivy on its own is dull as ground cover; interplant ivy with plants which flower at different times, for example snowdrops for early spring, narcissus for late spring, Turk's-cap lily for summer and speckled common Lords and Ladies for the fall. Bulbs can be planted with all low-lying ground-cover plants. For bulbs that like wet soil, moneywort can be used as a companion ground cover. Fill in with a couple of wintergreen ferns and the low-maintenance garden is complete and varied.

Protected bulbs in the wild

In addition to orchids and gentians and some other plants, a number of bulbous plants are protected in many countries. It is forbidden to dig up and remove these plants. In fact, it is not necessary to do so, as there are sufficient natural plant nurseries for the indigenous plants and specialist bulb suppliers, including the better garden centers, where these plants can be bought. Bulbous plants attract most attention when flowering and this is the worst time to dig them up and take them away. Of course different protection regulations apply specifically for each country, but the following bulbous plants are protected in most countries:

A fine little plant for the rockery is Cyclamen coum; *even when not flowering, its marbled foliage is a delight to behold.*

Lords and ladies	*Arum maculatum*
Turk's-cap lily	*Lilium martagon*
Wild hyacinth	*Hyacinthoides bifolia*
Dog's-tooth violet	*Erythronium dens-canis*
Snake's-head fritillary	*Fritillaria meleagris*
Wild tulip	*Tulipa sylvestris*
Summer snowflake	*Leucojum aestivum*
Spring snowflake	*L. vernum*
Poet's narcissus	*Narcissus poeticus*
Marsh gladiolus	*Gladiolus palustre*
Cyclamen	*Cyclamen purpurascens* (syn. *C. europaeum*)

Regrettably, bulbous plants, primarily snowdrops and cyclamen, are being taken commercially in great quantities from the wild in Greece and Turkey. This practice has given bulb dealers a bad name. It seems that this occupation will continue to be worthwhile, certainly so long as the buying public continues to be unaware of what is going on or does not buy discerningly. When you buy bulbs, pay attention to whether they are of cultivated origin.

Indigenous bulbous plants

When laying out a native garden it is necessary to know which plants are indigenous in origin. Many bulbous plants have been introduced and subsequently naturalized, and many of these are now described as indigenous plants, more properly naturalized plants. Below is a list of species which cannot be accepted as being native anywhere in North America.

Allium ursinum	wild or bear's garlic
A. schoenoprasum	chives
A. oleraceum	field garlic
A. vineale	crow garlic
A. scorodoprasum	sand leek
Colchicum autumnale	meadow saffron
Fritillaria meleagris	wild snake's-head fritillary
Gagea lutea	yellow star of Bethlehem
G. pratensis	
G. spathacea	
G. villosa	
Leucojum aestivum	summer snowflake
L. vernum	spring snowflake
Lilium bulbiferum subsp. *croceum*	orange lily
Narcissus pseudonarcissus subs. *pseudonarcissus*	wild daffodil, Lent lily
Ornithogalum umbellatum	common star of Bethlehem
Scilla non-scripta	English bluebell

Leucojum vernum *is one of the protected plants.*

TIP

Rabbits can constitute a real pest in the garden but they do not ordinarily nibble on the following plants. Remember, though, that if they are really hungry, they will even consume these plants. Garden lovers will always put chicken wire around their garden if it is in an area overrun with rabbits. The chicken wire need not be very high, but must be well dug in in places.

Agapanthus
Anemone
Colchicum
Convallaria
Crinum
Crocosmia
Cyclamen
Geranium tuberosum
Iris
Leucojum
Trillium

Combinations with other plants

Most bulbous plants combine well with permanent plants. Plant the early spring plants with permanent plants which come up later: a bed with rhubarb, for example, can be livened up with *Iris sibirica, Puschkinia* or the common winter aconite. There are also permanent plants which die back early and in such cases the tufts of the madonna lily are not unbecoming. Bulbous plants are also suitable for the bare ground under shrubs. A disadvantage of this is that the dead bulb foliage has to be cleared away if the shrub does not grow sufficiently to hide it.

The early-flowering yellow *Cornus mas* combines well with the early-flowering double narcissus 'Texas'. Yellow is, after all, a real spring color, particularly for those people who like to arrange their garden in single-colored drifts.

Most bulbous plants look attractive between low-lying ground-cover plants. Where permanent plants are involved, be careful to ensure that the flowers are not overgrown by the foliage of permanent plants that appear early. Yellow, white, blue, and violet are the most common colors in spring plants, and it is not difficult to think of good color combinations. The case is somewhat different with summer bulbs, where all the colors of the rainbow can be found. As there are few permanent plants with red flowers, the red and orange hues of the bulb flowers are a welcome addition here.

A river of grape hyacinths.

The short-stemmed tulips are coming up between the pansies. The pansy and forget-me-not are the plants most usually combined with tulips.

Combinations of biennials and bulb flowers have become almost standard: yellow narcissi between dark red wallflowers; a bed of red tulips interspersed with blue forget-me-nots; hyacinths and tulips in a bed spruced up with winter pansies; late narcissi combined with honesty – there is no end to the possibilities. Combinations can be made in pots between different types of bulbous plants. Pansies can always be used for underplanting. An Italian Arum can be combined with a hosta in a pot which is going to stay outside in winter. When the arum lily dies back, the hosta begins to grow nicely. The same applies with peonies and meadow saffron: the peony has practically died back when the meadow saffron flowers appear.

This combination is attractive even in spring, when the meadow saffron leaf appears quite early. Plan according to when a particular plant is at its least beautiful and which bulbous plant reaches its peak at that particular time.

Flower containers with dwarf conifers can be enlivened by tulips from the *greigii, fosteriana* and *kaufmanniana* groups. The foliage of these tulips is also attractive.

The use of bulb flowers can be seen each spring in many public gardens, especially botanical gardens, where plants will usually be labeled so that appealing combinations can be noted. Many such displays are developed around themes which with a little thought can be adapted to private gardens, large or small.

Hyacinthoides hispanica *combined with the dark green of* Hedera helix.

Spring-Flowering Bulbous and Tuberous Plants

In this chapter and in the ones which follow, you will find the choices listed in columns giving the color, flowering period, and height in inches (cm) of the plant in question.

Anemone blanda *'White Splendour', the hardiest and largest of the early spring anemones.*

Bulb availability varies each year. The trade does not depend solely on the domestic market, but demand from abroad also determines the price and, in part, the range. If it is fashionable in Japan to buy light blue flowers this year, you will find few *Muscari azureum* in the shops, while it will be possible to get bright blue grape hyacinths aplenty. The availability or scarcity of a specific plant does not depend solely on the grower, but also upon the "trend."

It is astonishing how many cheap small bulbs there are now which are little-known. Lesser known bulbous plants need not be expensive. Buy these small plants in large quantities so they will clearly make their mark in the garden.

The flowering periods given in catalogs depend to a great extent on the winter temperature and late frosts, but also on the region where you live. In colder parts of North America, the earliest spring bulbs are sure to flower two, or even three months later on average than in the southern parts of the continent. The latest spring-flowering bulbs, for example *Narcissus poeticus* var. *recurvus*, flower more closely together regardless of zone. In cooler climates, the total flowering period for spring-flowering plants is therefore shorter than is suggested in the catalogs.

***Allium* (Liliaceae), onion**

Nearly all the 300 allium species belong to the latest spring-flowering plants; some are still in flower in the summer. Plant them not too shallowly in a site in full sun. The soil must be lime-rich or neutral and must not be too damp. Often the foliage is not very pretty, so combine alliums with permanent plants which will conceal their foliage. Unattractive foliage can also be removed while the plant is in flower. A number of species are not very attractive in the garden. An exception to this is the wild, or bear's, garlic, *A. ursinum*, an excellent ground-cover plant, with the added advantage that its foliage dies back fully in July. The other small-bulb onions are also suitable for naturalization. *A. cepa* var. *viviparum* (tree onion or Egyptian onion) is a pretty onion for the vegetable garden. *A. schoenoprasum* is the well-known chive, also good for use in borders or as an edging plant, now also available in a mauve-red color. The flat-leaved Chinese chive (*A. tuberosum*) is more suited to the vegetable garden. The Welsh onion (*A. fistulosum*) also comes from China. Garlic and leek also belong to the allium genus. *A. aflatunense* and *A. atropurpureum* propagate themselves. *A. caeruleum, A. caesium, A. mairei, A. schubertii* and *A. zebdanense* are not fully winter-hardy. Plant these species in a site which is not too damp and cover them in winter. Plant all bulb alliums in November.

A. aflatunense	mauve/pink	end of May	32 in (80 cm)
A. albopilosum	mauve	May	20 in (50 cm)
A. angulosum	mauve-pink	June-Sept.	14 in (35 cm)
A. atropurpureum	aubergine	May	28 in (70 cm)

Allium cernuum *is one of the few ornamental onions that does not have a spherical flower.*

Allium rosenbachianum *'Album' is one of the larger ornamental onions which are suitable for a site between permanent plants in the border.*

A. caeruleum (A. azureum)	deep sky-blue	June	20 in (50 cm)
A. caesium (A. urseolatum)	violet blue		20 in (50 cm)
A. cernuum	mauve	July	12 in (30 cm)
A. christophii	silvery purple	May	12 in (30 cm)
A. cowanii	snow white	April-May	16 in (40 cm)
A. cyaneum	violet-blue	July	8 in (20 cm)
A. fistulosum	yellowy-white	May-June	24 in (60 cm)
A. flavum	golden yellow	July-August	12 in (30 cm)
A. giganteum	violet	July	4 ft (1.2 m)
A. karataviense	green/white	May	8 in (20 cm)
A. macleanii	mauve-purple	May-June	36 in (90 cm)
A. mairei	pale pink-dark red		4 in (10 cm)
A. maximowiczii	pink	April	8 in (20 cm)
A. moly (A. luteum)	yellow	June-July	8 in (20 cm)
A. narcissiflorum	purple	June-July	12 in (30 cm)
A. neapolitanum	bright white	April-May	12 in (30 cm)
A. nigrum	white, green center	June	28 in (70 cm)
A. oreophilum	purple	June-July	6 in (15 cm)
A. paradoxum	white, green specks	March-April	10 in (25 cm)
A. rosenbachianum	purple	May-June	24 in (60 cm)
A. r. 'Album'	white	May-June	24 in (60 cm)
A. roseum	white	June	12 in (30 cm)
A. schoenoprasum	purple	May-July	16 in (40 cm)
A. s. 'Albiflorum'	pale pink to white	May-July	16 in (40 cm)
A.s. 'Forescate'	deep purply-red	May-July	12 in (30 cm)
A. schubertii	maroon	May	18 in (45 cm)
A. siculum	browny-green	June	24 in-3 ft (60 cm–1 m)
A. sphaerocephalon	purply-red	July	16 in (40 cm)
A. stipitatum	dark pink	July	4½ ft (1.4 m)
A. s. 'Album'	white	July	4½ ft (1.4 m)
A. triquetrum	white, pendent	May-June	20 in (50 cm)
A. tuberosum	silvery white	July-Sept.	16 in (40 cm)
A. unifolium	soft pink	May-June	16 in (40 cm)
A. ursinum	white	May-June	12 in (30 cm)
A. zebdanense	white	April	10 in (25 cm)

The field garlic (*A. oleraceum*), sand leek (*A. scorodoprasum*), and crow garlic (*A. vineale*) are less attractive in gardens.

***Anemone* (Ranunculaceae), anemone**

A distinction is drawn here between tubers which flower in the early spring and larger tubers which flower later. These larger plants, *A. coronaria*, flower in April–May if planted in fall. They should be protected against frost when grown in colder regions by using a thick mulch of deciduous leaves. Other anemones, for example the wood anemone (*A. nemorosa*), have fine rhizomes. Do not allow these to dry out before planting. The rock-hard cormlets must be soaked for

De Caen-type Anemone *mixed, with vivid red* Anemone fulgens *in between. They are perhaps less appropriate in a formal garden, but a cottage garden is ideal.*

twenty-four hours before planting. *A. blanda* is usually supplied mixed. It is preferable, nevertheless, to buy single-color varieties, as growing method and flower size vary somewhat; there is a great risk that the white ones will dominate. The white *A. blanda* is 8 in (20 cm) high; the large-flowered variety is somewhat taller; all other varieties are shorter. They flower in April. Anemones are propagated vegetatively by breaking off the cormlets in pieces (I do not take permanent plant anemones into consideration here). *A. coronaria* can also be planted in the spring, and its flowering period will be July–August.

Tubers, with small flowers:

A. apennina	bright blue	March–April	4 in (10 cm)
A. a. var. *alba*	pale blue, white inside	March–April	4 in (10 cm)
A. blanda 'Blue Shades'	various blues		
A. b. 'Charmer'	deep red		
A. b. 'Pink Star'	pinky-purple		
A. b. 'Radar'	purply-red, white center		
A. b. 'Rosea'	cyclamen purple		
A. b. 'Violet Star'	violet, white center		
A. b. 'White Splendour'	white, large flower		

Tubers, large-flowered:

A. coronaria	large flowered:		
De Caen type,	single-flowered,	April–May	10 in (25 cm)

The color, flowering period, and site of Anemone ranunculoides *are the same as those for pilewort, for which reason it is often difficult to differentiate between them.*

A. c. 'The Bride'	white		
A. c. 'Hollandia'	red		
A. c. 'Mr. Fokker'	violet-blue		
A. c. 'Sylphide'	pinky-purple, dark center, double-flowered	April–May	10 in (25 cm)
A. c. 'King of the Blues'	dark blue		
A. c. 'Lord Derby'	violet-blue		
A. c. 'Lord Lieutenant'	deep blue, semi-double		
A. c. 'Mount Everest'	white, semi-double		
A. c. 'Surprise'	red		
A. c. 'The Admiral'	purple		
A. c. 'The Governor'	red, dark center		
A. c. 'Queen of the Violets'	purple		
A. fulgens	scarlet, single	April–May	10 in (25 cm)
	with rhizome, flowering period	March–April	
A. nemorosa	white, soft pink on the outside		
A. n. 'Alba Plena'	white, double		
A. n. 'Allenii'	blue, large-flowered		
A. n. 'Grandiflora'	white, large-flowered		
A. n. 'Robinsoniana'	pale blue		

A. blanda *'White Splendour' is much larger than* A. nemorosa, *the wild wood anemone.*

A. n. 'Rosea'	pink
A. n. 'Royal Blue'	dark blue
A. n. 'Vendobonensis'	cream
A. ranunculoides	dark yellow
A. r. 'Superba'	bronze-green foliage
A. r. 'Flore Pleno'	double flower
A. r. 'Wockeana'	yellow, smaller all over

***Arisarum* (Araceae), mouseplant**

This ground-cover plant, suitable for light shade and soil with a high humus content, has small dark green leaves which are reminiscent of the arum lily. This plant even used to be classified under the *Arum* genus. Small green berries appear in the fall.

A. proboscideum	chestnut	March–April 8 in(20 cm)

***Arum* (Araceae), arum**

The common dragon arum is a good hardy plant with arrow-shaped leaves, between which a large dark red flower with a black spadix unfurls. A smell of dung attracts the insects necessary for pollination. The garden arums have fleshy rhizomes. The foliage appears in the fall and dies back again in spring, a cycle that is the reverse of the hosta's, which is why they make a perfect combination. Vivid orange spikes of berries appear after July, earlier in the case of *A. maculatum*, somewhat later in the case of *A. italicum*. The plants tolerate deep shade under leafy trees on soil with a high organic content and preferably lime-rich, and are poisonous.

A. maculatum and others are imported and often naturalized. These plants will also tolerate severe drought in summer. *A. dioscorides* needs protection in winter. *Arum dracunculus*: see *Dracunculus vulgaris*.

A. creticum	creamy yellow	April–May	16 in (40 cm)
A. dioscorides	green, purple spikes, spotted with purple	April	16 in (40 cm)
A. italicum	greeny white	April–May	16 in (40 cm)
A. i. 'Marmoratum'	*idem*, light green-veined leaf		
A. maculatum	*idem*, speckled leaf	April–May	16 in (40 cm)

Babiana (Iridaceae)

This tender small plant flowers in late spring. It is named after the baboon which, in South Africa, where the plant grows naturally, eats it whenever it can find the corm. Plant them relatively deep, about 6 in (15 cm). At the same time, give them a warm sunny site. They are also suitable for growing in pots. Overwinter them in a frost-free place.

B. stricta 'Purple Star'	reddish purple	May	12–16 in (30–40 cm)
B. s. 'Tubergen's Blue'	purple, white spots	April–May	16 in (40 cm)

It is not the flowers of the arum which are the most spectacular, but the spikes of berries which stand leafless above the ground in late summer.

Chionodoxa luciliae.

Begonia (Begoniaceae), hardy tuberous begonia Only begonia which originate from China are winter-hardy, provided they are well-protected against frost. Provide a warm site, but not in full sun. Give them well-drained soil to prevent rotting in damp winters. It is better to grow them in pots, as they can be placed inside in a cool place for the winter. This plant can easily be propagated by planting out the bulblets which are formed in the leaf axils.

B. grandis	pale pink	July–Sept.	12 in (30 cm)
B. g. 'Alba'	white	July–Sept.	12 in (30 cm)

Bellevalia (Liliaceae) This plant, which resembles the grape hyacinth, is also easy to grow and requires roughly the same conditions: dry and sunny. Earlier names are *Muscari paradoxum* and *Muscari pycnantha*.

B. pycnantha	blackish-blue	May	8 in (20 cm)
B. romana	white, blue tips	April	12 in (30 cm)

Bongardia (Berberidaceae) This plant originates from Syria and Iran. It must be cared for in the same way as *Begonia grandis*. Plant this expensive bulbous plant 8 in (20 cm) deep to avoid frost damage, in full sun.

B. chrysogonum	golden yellow	March–May	12 in (30 cm)

Brimeura (Liliaceae) This little-known plant, which is, however, easy to grow, looks like a miniature bluebell. *B. fastigiata* is so small – 2 in (5 cm) – that it is better to put it in a protected place in a cold greenhouse. This genus used to be called *Hyacinthus*. An alpine plant from the Pyrenees that has been cultivated since 1600, it tolerates both sun and shade.

B. amethystina	pale to deep blue	March–June	6–8 in (15–20 cm)
B. a. 'Alba'	white	May	8 in (20 cm)

Brodiaea (Liliaceae) The cut flower brings to mind the Agapanthus. Give it moist, well-drained soil in full to half shade. Protect it well from frost.

B. californica	blue-violet	June	28 in (70 cm)

Bulbocodium (Liliaceae) The leaf of this crocus-like plant appears after the flower. It is not the easiest garden plant to grow. Put it in a sunny site with well-drained soil. In growers' catalogs, it is often included under the fall-flowering plants, as the planting time is similar to that of the meadow saffron. The foliage appears just as the flower is finishing.

B. vernum	red-purply violet	March–April	4 in (10 cm)

Camassia (Liliaceae) quamash This bulbous plant, which originates from the western United States, fits in well with the permanent plant border and can naturalize. It requires a damp to wet site, rich soil, and full sun. It is best propagated by seed in a lightly shaded site. It should be planted roughly 6 in (15 cm) apart, rather less for *C. quamash*, rather more for the others.

C. cusickii	sky blue	June–July	24 in (60 cm)
C. c. 'Zwanenburg'	pale blue	June–July	24 in (60 cm)
C. leichtlinii 'Alba'	white	June–July	32 in (80 cm)
C. l. 'Caerulea'	pale blue	June–July	32 in (80 cm)
C. l. 'Plena'	white, semi-double	June–July	32 in (80 cm)
C. quamash (*C. esculenta*)	pale violet-blue	June–July	16 in (40 cm)
C. q. 'Orion'	dark violet-blue	June–July	16 in (40 cm)

Camassia quamash.

Chionodoxa (Liliaceae), glory of the snow Plant these early flowerers right by the house, so that you can see them well. They are suitable for naturalization, as underplanting, and in the rock garden. They originate from the high mountain regions of Asia Minor. They are 6 in (15 cm) high and are not very demanding.

C. forbesii	blue, white center	March–April	6 in (15 cm)
C. luciliae	lavender, white center	March	
C. l. 'Alba'	brilliant white	March	
C. l. 'Blue Giant'	blue	March	
C. l. 'Pink Giant'	soft pinkish-violet	March	
C. l. 'Rosea'	pinky-violet	March	
C. l. 'Zwanenburg'	blue, white center	March	
C. sardensis	gentian blue	March	

x _Chionoscilla_ (Liliaceae) This bigeneric (i.e., from two different genera) hybrid between *Chionodoxa* and *Scilla* constitutes a botanical rarity called x *C. allenii*, which is rarely in cultivation.

Anyone who does not like staking must pay careful attention to height when buying dahlias: this low-growing white Topmix dahlia does not need any support.

Colchicum (Liliaceae)

An exception among the meadow saffrons: leaf and flower appear at the same time in early spring. This Asiatic plant has several light to dark yellow flowers on each stem. As for the other colchicums, the planting time is in August and September.

C. luteum	yellow	Jan.–March	4 in (10 cm)

Corydalis (Papaveraceae), holewort, fumewort

C. bulbosa and *C. solida* are very similar. The former (holewort) is best propagated by seed, and the latter (fumewort) by dividing the clumps with pretty round bulblets.

These species are extremely suitable for naturalization under trees and shrubs. After a few years they will form a carpet of flowers. Their bulbs look very different. The holewort has large bulbs with a hollow on the underside and the fumewort has small round bulblets. They need humus-rich soil and are one of the few naturalizing bulbs which also do well in sandy soil. The following species all flower reasonably early.

C. angustifolia	white	March–April	8 in (20 cm)
C. bulbosa (C. cava)	pinky-purple or white	April	12 in (30 cm)
C. decipiens	violet-red	March	12 in (30 cm)
C. diphyla	white with purple	April	4 in (10 cm)
C. solida	pale mauve	March–April	10 in (25 cm)

***Crocus* (Iridaceae), crocus**

A distinction can be made here between fall-flowering and spring-flowering crocus. Some of the eighty species are vigorous self-propagators: the fall-flowering *C. speciosus* and the spring-flowering *C. tomasinianus*. The spring crocus *C. vernus*, which looks like an "ordinary" crocus, self-propagates to a lesser extent. Buy crocuses in large numbers, in single colors or mixed. Try to create a smooth transition between the colors, for example from dark colors next to a tree trunk to light ones further away from the trunk. Scatter the bulbs in single colors and swap some bulbs around where the different colors meet. The clearly-defined border will become indistinct and there will be a gradual change of color. *C. sativus* can be planted in the herb garden – the stamens provide saffron. Fall flowering crocuses must be planted as early as July. They can usually be obtained only from specialist bulb dealers.

Crocus chrysanthus *'Fuscotinctus'.*

Small-flowered species and varieties:

C. ancyrensis 'Golden Bunch'	orange, early
C. angustifolius	deep orange, reddish brown on outside
C. a. 'Minor'	golden yellow, violet-brown stripe, early
C. chrysanthus 'Advance'	yellow with bronze, mauveish outside
C. c. 'Blue Bird'	white, gray-blue outside
C. c. 'Blue Pearl'	silvery blue, pale blue outside
C. c. 'Blue Peter'	purple-blue with yellow center
C. c. 'Buttercup'	golden yellow, brown inside
C. c. 'Cream Beauty'	creamy yellow, purple stripes
C. c. 'Elegance'	lemon yellow, gray-brown outside, yellow edge
C. c. 'E.P. Bowles'	lemon yellow
C. c. 'Eyecatcher'	snow white, blue specks, outside deep purple with white edge
C. c. 'Fuscotinctus'	lemon yellow, brown stripe
C. c. 'Gipsy Girl'	bronze-colored, striped
C. c. 'Goldilocks'	deep yellow
C. c. 'Jeannine'	creamy yellow, outside pale purple
C. c. 'Ladykiller'	violet-purple with white edge
C. c. 'Prins Claus'	white, violet-speckled outside
C. c. 'Princess Beatrix'	light blue, golden yellow center
C. c. 'Snowbunting'	white, purple-striped outside
C. c. 'White Triumphater'	brilliant white, soft yellow center
C. c. 'Zwanenburg Bronze'	bronze-colored, yellow inside
C. corsicus	dark mauve, outside striped
C. etruscus 'Zwanenburg'	purple-blue, violet-veined outside
C. korolkowii	golden yellow, outside speckled brown purple
C. minimus	purple, outside yellowish and violet-veined
C. sieberi 'Bowles White'	silver-white, yellow center

C. s. 'Firefly'	violet-pink, gray flush
C. s. 'Violet Queen'	pale violet, yellow base, darker outside
C. stellaris	golden yellow, outside striped mauve
C. tomasinianus	pale lavender blue
C. t. 'Albus'	silvery-white
C. t. 'Barr's Purple'	violet-pink
C. t. 'Pictus'	lavender, purple specks
C. t. 'Roseus'	bright pink, outside gray flush
C. t. 'Ruby Giant'	ruby-purple
C. t. 'Whitewell Purple'	reddish violet
C. vernus	all colors
C. versicolor	white, fine purple stripes
'Picturatus' syn. *C. versicolor* 'Cloth of Gold'	
Large-flowered varieties:	
C. 'Blue Pearl'	blue
C. 'Jeanne d'Arc'	white
C. 'King of the Striped'	blue, striped
C. 'Peter Pan'	white
C. 'Pickwick'	silvery-gray with mauve-blue stripe
C. 'Purpureus Grandiflorus'	purple-blue
C. 'Remembrance'	purple-blue
C. 'Vanguard'	mauve, outside gray-blue, early

Crocus tomasinianus *'Ruby Giant' is stronger in color than the wild species and is also easier to obtain.*

Crocus tomasinianus *is the best crocus for naturalizing.*

C. 'Yellow Mammoth'	deep yellow		

The large-flowered 'Remembrance' crocus is the most common garden crocus and the best for growing indoors.

Dichelostemma (Liliaceae)

This plant genus is classified under both the onion and the lily family. It is closely related to *Brodiaea* and used to have that name. It needs well-drained soil and a warm sunny site. It needs protection in winter. It is perhaps more advisable to grow it in a cold greenhouse or in pots. It can be propagated by seed or by planting out the bulblets. The special *D. volubile* has twining flower stalks which need support – perhaps a small shrub? The others have long leafless stems which do not require support. The species comes from California; a bit of warmth is therefore desirable. In comparison with other bulbous plants, they flower for a long time.

D. congestum	dark violet	June–July	32 in (80 cm)
D. ida-maia	red, green edge	June	20 in (50 cm)
D. volubile	pink	May	32 in (80 cm)

Dracunculus (Araceae), common dragon arum

Synonym: *Arum dracunculus*. The plant is hardy, but protect it in winter nevertheless. I would recommend keeping it out of frost. It can be grown on its own in a woodland corner or in a tub, although the rank smell does not justify a place on the patio. The plant is still widely sold under the name of *Arum*, which it brings to mind, although this is much larger.

The tubers should preferably be planted in partial shade in spring.

D. vulgaris	red/black	May–June	32 in (80 cm)

***Eranthis* (Ranunculaceae), winter aconite**

These early-flowering plants, ideal for lawns, are not much bothered by frost and snow. They can spread vigorously on clay soil and will even grow on gravel paths. Collected seed must be re-sown immediately. The "shapeless" hard small tubers must be soaked before planting. Plant them relatively deep: 6 in (15 cm). *E. cilicica* has larger flowers and deeply incised leaves.

E. cilicica	yellow	March	4 in (10 cm)
E. hyemalis	yellow	February	4 in (10 cm)

Eranthis hyemalis *is one of the few bulbous plants which is not out of place in a heather garden.*

***Eremurus* (Liliaceae), foxtail lily**

Young plants are tender, so cover them in winter and plant them in a sunny, sandy site. The plants have long fleshy rhizomes. Put this plant between medium-high permanent plants, so that the less attractive foliage is hidden from view. Plant the bulb with the tip almost on the surface and let the roots spread as they are when you buy the plant. These flowers are recommended for cutting, but I haven't the heart to cut off the candles of flowers that look so stately in the garden.

New varieties in cultivation are *E.* 'Himrob' (soft pink), *E.* 'Obelisk' (white, green center), and *E.* 'Pinokkio' (yellow, orange stamens).

E. aitchisonii	pale pink	May–June	6 ft (2 m)
E. 'Cleopatra'	orange/dark red	June	4½ ft (1.4 m)
E. himalaicus	white	May–June	36 in (90 cm)
E. olgae	soft pink	July–Aug.	3 ft (1 m)
E. robustus	soft pink	August	8 ft (2.5 m)

The nomenclature of Eremurus *is rather confusing. The name* E. bungei *has now been changed to* E. stenophyllus.

***Erythronium* (Liliaceae), dog's-tooth violet**

This easy tuberous plant deserves to be used more. Plant it proportionately quite deep and protect it in winter. Do not let it dry out: plant the corms as soon as you get them or keep them in damp peat. The bright green leaves are delightfully speckled and veined. The shape of the corms is reminiscent of a dog's eye-tooth.

E. californicum 'White Beauty'	white, leaf yellow veins	April–May	8 in (20 cm)
E. dens-canis	white, pink or purple, speckled leaf	March	12 in (30 cm)
E. d. 'Rose Queen'	brown speckled leaf	April	4 in (10 cm)
E. hendersonii	blue-violet, light green speckled leaf	April	12 in (30 cm)
E. 'Pagoda'	sulfur-yellow, bronze leaf, speckled	April–May	12 in (30 cm)
E. tuolumnense	golden yellow, leaf shiny green	April–May	12 in (30 cm)

***Ferraria* (Iridaceae)**

In the wild, it grows in sandy soil in South Africa. The leaves surround the stems, which makes them reminiscent of spathes. Give this small plant a warm sunny site in the rock garden.

F. crispa	brown-purple with greeny-white	July	10 in (25 cm)

Fritillaria **(Liliaceae), crown imperial, snake's-head fritillary**

Nearly all fritillaries flower in April or May. Give them a damp site. The bulbs must not dry out, so plant them immediately. The name crown imperial refers to the seed capsules; although the flowers are pendulous, the seed capsules stand erect and together they form a crown. Moles are said to stay a few feet (meters) away from the bulbs, but to say that the bulbs drive out moles is an overstatement. The characteristic, penetrating smell of the bulb and flower can be detected even from a great distance. Plant the bulbs deep – 8 in (20 cm) – so that summer flowers can be planted above the bulbs. In the fall, in frost-free regions, pansies can be planted in the same bed, so that it is in flower both summer and winter. The snake's-head fritillary, *F. meleagris*, can be planted in a damp ditch wall or in a very moist lawn which will be mown for the first time late in the spring. With crown imperials, blind flower shoots can sometimes be produced; the 'Fasciata' variety with brown-red flowers is grown with this in mind. The species of *F. minuta* (browny-orange), *montana* (dark purple), *stenanthera* (soft pink, dark center), and *stribrnyi* (very deep purple, red with yellow stripe inside), are expensive bulbs for enthusiasts. These are only a few of the 125 species that occur in the wild in

Erythronium californicum *'White Beauty' (in the photo) and* Erythronium *'Pagoda' are the most commonly grown.*

The bulb of Fritillaria imperialis *is perennial. On the top the gap is where the flower stem was the previous year.*

Europe, North Africa, Asia, and North America. Although the species mentioned are hardy, it is advisable to cover them in winter.

F. acmopetala	green and brown, olive-green inside	April–May	16 in (40 cm)
F. affinis	dark purple	April	20 in (50 cm)
F. assyriaca	brown, yellow edge		16 in (40 cm)
F. biflora 'Martha Roderick'	browny-red, light green spots	April–May	10 in (25 cm)
F. brandegei	purple-pink	April–May	12 in (30 cm)
F. camtschatcensis	off-white	April–May	10 in (25 cm)
F. davisii	chocolate brown	April	6 in (15 cm)
F. graeca	greenish, brown-speckled tops	April	8 in (20 cm)
F. imperialis	red, white-edged leaf		5 ft (1.5 m)
F. i. 'Aureomarginata'	red, creamy yellow-edged leaf		
F. i. 'Aurora'	orange-red		
F. i. 'Fasciata'	browny-red, produces blind flower shoots		32 in (80 cm)
F. i. 'Lutea Maxima'	yellow		3 ft (1 m)
F. i. 'Premier'	orange-red, purple flush		
F. i. 'Prolifera'	orange-red, two crowns		32 in (80 cm)
F. i. 'Rubra Maxima'	red/orange		3 ft (1 m)
F. involucrata	gray-green	April	

F. meleagris	mixed colors	March–May	8 in (20 cm)
F. m. 'Alba'	white		8 in (20 cm)
F. m. 'Jupiter'	purple-red with red veins, large		14 in (35 cm)
F. m. 'Mars'	purple, large		10 in (25 cm)
F. michailovskyi	red-brown, yellow edge	April	4 in (10 cm)
F. pallidiflora	pale yellow, blue-green leaf		12 in (30 cm)
F. persica	deep purple		3 ft (1 m)
F. p. 'Adiyaman'	purple	April	3 ft (1 m)
F. pontica	green, light brown specks		12 in (30 cm)
F. uva-vulpis see *F. assyriaca*			
F. verticillata	cream, green-veined		24 in (60 cm)

The snake's-head fritillary is usually supplied mixed. If you want a single color, label the white ones, so that they can be planted together after flowering.

Gagea (Liliaceae), star of Bethlehem

Listed below are four examples of the star of Bethlehem. All are indigenous, but only *G. lutea* is known in the bulb trade. They like clay soil and even do well on heavy clay. In country estates, parks and public gardens, they often grow *en masse* in lawns. Grass-like taller tufts appear in among the grass and star-shaped flowers appear only when the plant begins to die back. It is also suitable for the border and the rock garden provided the site is moisture-retentive even in the summer. The special *G. graeca*, whose flowers do not open into a star shape, requires the warmth of at least a cold greenhouse and likes dry ground.

Geranium tuberosum, commonly called the cranesbill.

G. villosa	yellow	March–April	8 in (20 cm)
G. spathacea	yellow	March–April	8 in (20 cm)
G. pratensis	yellow	March–April	4 in (10 cm)
G. lutea	yellow	March–April	8 in (20 cm)

Galanthus (Liliaceae), Snowdrop

To prevent the bulbs drying out in the summer, when they are dormant, they must be planted relatively deep: 6 in (15 cm), preferably in partial shade. In some places, the snowdrop spreads *en masse*. The first ones begin to flower again as early as the second year. It is easy to propagate them in the garden by carefully lifting and dividing the clumps while they are in flower. This should be done every two years. After a number of years, the garden will be full of them. Although snowdrops prefer lime-rich soil, they still do well on slightly acid soil. There are dozens of species, most of which are rarely sold. *G. nivalis* is common, and a number of varieties are in cultivation. *G. reginae-olgae* is an fall-flowering plant for a dry and sunny site. Snowdrops all have blue-green foliage; *G. ikariae* (syn. *G. latifolius)* is an exception to this, with its bright green foliage. For all snowdrops, the bulbs must not dry out above the ground. It is preferable to buy the more expensive species as small potted plants.

G. elwesii	white	Feb.–March	12 in (30 cm)
G. ikariae	white	March	14 in (35 cm)
G. nivalis	white	March	8 in (20 cm)

G. n. 'Atkinsii'	white	March	10 in (25 cm)
G. n. 'Flore Pleno'	white	Feb.–March	8 in (20 cm)
G. n. 'Lutescens'	white, small-flowered		
G. n. 'Viridi-apice'	white, green tips	Feb.–March	6 in (15 cm)

Geranium (Geraniaceae), tuberous cranesbill

Plant these fleshy rhizomes in well-drained soil that is not too moist, in partial shade. This hardy genus includes hundreds of species, most of which are classed as permanent plants; some are indigenous, but this does not apply to the rhizome plants listed below. Tuberous cranesbills occur in the wild in Spain.

G. tuberosum	pink/pale purple	April–June	10 in (25 cm)
G. malviflorum	dark mauve	June	12 in (30 cm)

*The most common snowdrop (*Galanthus nivalis*) is not bothered by a layer of snow and also grows well through a layer of well-rotted beech leaves.*

Gynandriris (Iridaceae), Barbary nut

The flowers of this bulbous plant, which looks like the iris, open in the afternoon and fade by the next morning. The flowers appear at different heights on the flower stem. The species listed below comes from the Mediterranean area. Put them in a sunny site; apart from that they are not very demanding.

G. sisyrinchium	dark blue, white specks	May–June	24 in (60 cm)

Hermodactylus (Iridaceae)

This rapidly spreading plant resembles the iris. It even used to be called *Iris tuberosa*. Plant them in the fall in a very sunny, sandy, well-drained site. These plants have a tuberous root stock.

H. tuberosus	dark purple-brown	April–May	12 in (30 cm)

Homeria (Iridaceae)

Although it comes from South Africa, the homeria is completely frost-hardy. Give it a sunny site that is not too damp.

H. collina	orange and yellow	June–July	20 in (50 cm)
H. ochroleuca	yellow	May–June	20 in (50 cm)

Hyacinthella (Liliaceae)

See *Muscari* and *Bellevalia*. The plant resembles them closely, except for the flowers, which are rather more open.

H. pallens	azure blue	April	4 in (10 cm)

Hyacinthoides (Liliaceae), wild hyacinth, harebell, bluebell

It is hard to tell from the potato-like tubers which is the top, it does no harm to plant them on their sides. Wild hyacinths are often sold under the names of *Scilla campanulata* and *Endymion hispanicus*. The most genuine "bluebell" is *H. non-scripta*, recognizable from the small flowers that hang from only one side of the stem. In the case of *H. hispanica*, the flowers are situated at random on the stem, as with the hyacinth. Many hybrids between these first-rate bulbs are appearing for propagation. In view of the late flowering period (May–June), it is usually not advisable to plant them in grass because of mowing, although the flower stems, which grow up to 16 in (40 cm) high, are sure to rise far above the long grass. Give them a moist, shady site. They are often supplied mixed; by buying single colors, it is

'Bismarck' hyacinth. When planting the pansies, you should already be thinking of the color combination: dark purple or light blue could have intensified the color of these

possible to make combinations yourself, although they are all in pastel shades which go well with each other.

H. hispanica		May–June	16 in (40 cm)
H. h. 'Blue Queen'	lavender blue		
H. h. 'Dainty Maid'	purple-pink		
H. h. 'Danube'	dark blue		
H. h. 'Excelsior'	deep lavender blue		
H. h. 'Queen of the Pinks'	deep pink		
H. h. 'Rosabella'	soft pink		
H. h. 'Rose Queen'	dark pink		
H. h. 'White City'	silvery-white		
H. h. 'White Queen'	white, smaller		
H. non-scripta	blue	May	12 in (30 cm)

***Hyacinthus* (Liliaceae), hyacinth**

The hyacinth is a bulbous plant suitable for flower beds and edging. Plant about fifty bulbs per square yard (square meter) 4 in (10 cm) deep. Before planting, keep the bulbs at room temperature. Wear gloves when planting, as the bulbs cause itching.

About 2,000 different varieties have come into existence, most of which have been lost again. You can propagate your favorites by cutting a shallow star in the base of the bulb using a sharp kitchen knife: young bulblets will appear there that will likely flower after three years. The multiflora hyacinths flower with several stems at

'Ostara' hyacinth.

once. These can be left in the ground. The ancestor of the varieties mentioned below is *H. orientalis*, a bluish-flowering species from South East Europe and Asia Minor. This natural species, which can no longer be compared with the single and double forms, is still on the market: true red, purple, and yellow. There are about twenty new varieties of double hyacinths on the market. The current traditional range is given below.

H. 'Amethyst'	violet-mauve	
H. 'Amsterdam'	deep pink with darker center	
H. 'Anne Marie'*	soft pink	early
H. 'Blue Giant'	light blue	
H. 'Blue Jacket'*	dark blue, purple stripe	
H. 'Blue Magic'	blue-purple, white center, large	
H. 'Carnegie'*	white	early
H. 'City of Haarlem'	pale yellow	reasonably early
H. 'Delfts Blauw'*	light blue	early
H. 'Fürst Bismarck'	light blue	very early
H. 'Gipsy Queen'	orange	
H. 'Hollyhock'	deep crimson red, double	
H. 'Jan Bos'*	reddish, white center	
H. 'Lady Derby'	pink	late
H. 'L'Innocence'*	white	
H. 'Lord Balfour'	violet	late
H. 'Maria Christina'	apricot	
H. 'Mulberry Rose'	pink, dark flower stem	
H. 'Ostara'*	blue-purple	early
H. 'Pink Pearl'*	pink	
H. 'Pink Surprise'	uniform pink	
H. 'Prins Hendrik'	all light yellow	early
H. 'Violet Pearl'	deep violet	
H. 'White Giant'	white, yellow stamen	

* = suitable for indoor temperatures

Ipheion (Liliaceae)

This is one of the cheapest bulbous plants, which are nevertheless little used; are you going to change that? They are low-growing little plants with pale green foliage that smells of onions. The flowers look steely-blue. This plant, which is native to South America, is still sold under the name of *Brodiaea*, but the names of *Milla* and *Triteleia* have also been in fashion. They will propagate themselves rapidly on a sunny site.

I. uniflorum	pale violet-blue	May–June	10 in (25 cm)
I. u. 'Rolf Fiedler'	deep blue	April	6 in (15 cm)
I. u. 'Wisley Blue'	light blue	May	8 in (20 cm)

Iris (Iridaceae)

There are irises which are spring-flowering bulbous plants, summer flowering bulbs and permanent plants. Of the spring-flowering bulbs, *I. danfordiae* and *I. reticulata* are remarkable because of their very early flowering. A must for every garden! Plant them close together to enable the low-growing small plants – 8 in (20 cm) – to come out well. The foliage stays standing beautifully erect and is therefore not annoying.

Early-flowering (Feb.–March), low-growing:

I. bakeriana	blue, yellow on violet tip
I. danfordiae	bright yellow
I. histrioides	deep blue
I. h. 'George'	purple, darker crest
I. h. 'Major'	deep blue
I. hyrcana	sky blue, yellow crest
I. reticulata 'Alba'	white
I. r. 'Alida'	sky blue, orange-yellow tip
I. r. 'Cantab'	light blue, orange crest
I. r. 'Clairette'	sky-blue, dark purple tip
I. r. 'Harmony'	cornflower blue, darker tip
I. r. 'Hercules'	velvety-purple, orange crest
I. r. 'Ida'	light blue, yellow crest, dark blue specks
I. r. 'Joyce'	bright blue, orange crest
I. r. 'J.S. Dijt'	purple-red, yellow crest
I. r. 'Natascha'	ivory white, green veined tip, golden yellow crest
I. r. 'Royal Blue'	dark purple blue, yellow crest

The 'Jan Bos' hyacinth has a particularly striking appearance, especially when the bulbs are planted close together in large groups.

The common species of Iris reticulata *is not the prettiest of spring irises: other varieties mentioned have more striking colors.*

I. r. 'Springtime'	blue, purple tip with white spots, yellow crest		
I. r. 'Violet Beauty'	violet, dark tip, orange crest		
Early-summer flowering varieties:			
I. bucharica	creamy white, tip with golden yellow specks		18 in (45 cm)
I. hoogiana	lavender blue	May	24 in (60 cm)
I. h. 'Alba'	white	May	20 in (50 cm)
I. magnifica	soft mauve		24 in (60 cm)
I. susiana	dark purple veins on lighter background		12 in (30 cm)

Iris *'Prof. Blaauw' is named after a bulb research scientist. It is not recommended for garden use: it is better to enjoy the cut flowers bought from the shop.*

Dutch Iris Crosses with *I. xiphioides* produced the "English" iris. Dutch crosses between *I. xiphium* (the Spanish iris), *I. tingitana,* and others are called Dutch irises *(Iris* x *hollandica).* These irises are specially treated under glass by growers as cut flowers. They are sensitive to both frost and wind and are therefore unsuitable for the garden. They can be grown well in the cut-flower patch in full sun. Stake them well: in good soil, they grow up to 32 in (80 cm) high. Plant them in fall 3 in (8 cm) deep in well-drained soil (to prevent frost damage), and cover them. Unfortunately, they are nearly always supplied in mixed packs for the garden.

I. 'Apollo'	light yellow with dark yellow

The official name for this Ixiolirion *is now* Ixiolirion tataricum *ssp* montanum.

I. 'Blue Champion'	blue
I. 'Bronze Queen'	bluish with bronze, yellow crest
I. 'Golden Emperor'	yellow
I. 'Lemon Queen'	lemon yellow
I. 'Paris'	dark blue-purple, yellow specks
I. 'Prof. Blaauw'	blue-purple, yellow crest
I. 'Saturnus'	creamy white with light yellow
I. 'Wedgewood'	light blue with orange-white
I. 'White Excelsior'	silver white, greeny-yellow striped tip

English irises This group of irises (*Iris latifolia*) comes from the damp meadows of the Pyrenees, but they have long been grown in England. They are 24 in (60 cm) high and the flowering period is June–July.

I. 'Delft Blue'	blue-violet veins
I. 'Duke of Clarence'	purple
I. 'Mont Blanc'	white

Spanish irises Spanish iris (*Iris xiphium*) is suitable as a cut flower and as a garden plant. Plant them fairly deep – 4–6in (10–15cm) to avoid frost damage. In the event of a late-night frost, cover them as they come up early. Cover them in winter to avoid frost damage. Height: 24 in (60 cm), flowering period: May–June.

I. 'Battandieri'	white, tips with yellow stripe

I. 'Koningin Wilhelmina'	white, tips with yellow specks, early
I. 'Lucitanica'	bronze-yellow
I. 'Thunderbolt'	purple-brown, tips bronze-yellow

***Ixiolirion* (Amaryllidaceae)**

This tender little plant can naturalize in a warm site. This plant also appears under the names of *I. ledebourii* and *I. palassii*, which can also be used for the species listed below. See *Ixia* for planting method and after-care.

I. montanum	bright blue	May-June	16 in (40 cm)
I. tataricum	deep blue	May-June	12 in (30 cm)

***Leucocoryne* (Liliaceae)**

Plant this special and tender plant from Chile in a sunny site, preferably in a cold greenhouse, although even there it must be protected.

L. purpurea	dark purple-violet	May–June	16 in (40 cm)

***Leucojum* (Amaryllidaceae), snowflake**

L. vernum, the spring snowflake, a name which is sometimes wrongly used for the later-flowering snowdrop, flowers even before the snowdrop. The shiny dark green foliage is striking. This bulbous plant requires damp, rich soil in partial shade. It produces foliage even in the winter months. The taller summer snowflake, *L. aestivum*, indigenous to west-central Europe, is rare and protected. Several bell-shaped flowers appear on a long stem. The clumps can be divided in

The summer snowflake proudly stands among the long, lush grass on the water's edge.

the spring or sown in fall. Put this plant in a very damp site; it likes to be in the water at times, even during the winter. Once bought, the bulbs must be kept moist or planted out immediately. The fall-flowering species, which are not so easily obtained, like full sun and must be well protected from frost. The late-summer-flowering *L. roseum* is suitable only for a cold greenhouse.

L. aestivum	white/green	April–May	10–14 in (25–35 cm)
L. a. 'Gravetye Giant'	white/green	May–June	16 in (40 cm)
L. autumnale	white	Sept.–Oct.	4–6 in (10–15 cm)
L. roseum	pale pink	Aug.–Sept.	4 in (10 cm)
L. valentinum	white	Sept.–Oct.	6 in (15 cm)
L. vernum	white	Feb.–March	8 in (20 cm)

***Lilium* (Liliaceae), lily**

Lilies must be planted fairly deep immediately on purchase. If kept dry, the fleshy scales of the bulb dry out too quickly, and if kept too wet, they rot quickly. This means that storing the bulbs is best left to nurserymen. *L. candidum*, the madonna or Maria lily, must not be planted too deep. This species and *L. martagon* like lime-rich soil; *L. speciosum* and *L. auratum* like acid soil. *L. bulbiferum* ssp *croceum* is the indigenous orange or rye lily. This lily can be obtained from genuine enthusiast nurserymen. Lilies are ideal border plants: the large flowers make their mark here and the permanent plants ensure that the sun cannot shine on the ground, so the soil stays cool. Both lilies and clematis do not like the sun to shine on the base of the stem. The following species are planted in October in moisture-retentive soil with a high organic content.

L. auratum	white, red specks	July	32 in (80 cm)
L. bulbiferum	orange-red		3 ft (1 m)
L. candidum	white	June	3 ft (1 m)
L. cernuum	soft purple-mauve	July	20 in (50 cm)
L. hansonii	golden yellow, brown-speckled leaf	July	3 ft (1 m)
L. henryi	orange	Aug.	4 ft (1.25 m)
L. lancifolium, see *L. tigrinum*			
L. martagon	brown-purple	June	3 ft (1 m)
L. m. var. *album*	white	June–July	3 ft (1 m)
L. pumilum	fiery red	July	24 in (60 cm)
L. pyrenaicum var. *aureum*	golden yellow, dark specks	May–June	4 ft (1.20 m)
L. regale	white, pink on outside	July	3 ft (1 m)
L. r. '*Album*'	white	July	3 ft (1 m)
L. x testaceum	yellow, red specks	June–July	3 ft (1 m)
L. tigrinum	orange-red, specks	July–Sept.	4 ft (1.25 m)

Lilium regale.

Muscari (Liliaceae), grape hyacinth

This is unjustly one of the most popular bulbous plants for the garden: the flower is magnificent, but the foliage, which is there for a long time, looks untidy. *M. armeniacum* and *M. botryoides* are among the cheapest bulbous plants available. Special-offer packets are largely filled with grape hyacinths. The best are *M. latifolium* and *M. neglectum*.

M. armeniacum	blue	March–April	8 in (20 cm)
M. a. 'Blue Spike'	blue, double	April–May	8 in (20 cm)
M. a. 'Cantab'	bright blue	April–May	4 in (10 cm)
M. a. 'Saffier'	dark blue	April–May	8 in (20 cm)
M. aucheri	blue to light blue	April–May	8 in (20 cm)
M. a. 'Dark Eyes'	azure blue	April–May	8 in (20 cm)
M. a. 'Sky Blue'	dark blue, light blue tip	April–May	8 in (20 cm)
M. a. 'White Beauty'	white, hint of pink	April–May	8 in (20 cm)
M. azureum	azure blue	March–April	6 in (15 cm)
M. a. 'Album'	white	March–April	6 in (15 cm)
M. botryoides 'Album'	white	April–May	8 in (20 cm)
M. comosum	soft violet blue	May–July	16 in (40 cm)
M. c. 'Plumosum'	violet blue	May–July	16 in (40 cm)
M. latifolium	pale blue/ dark blue	April	10 in (25 cm)

M. macrocarpum	brown-purple to yellowy-brown	April–May	8 in (20 cm)
M. muscarimi	soft yellow, purple tip	April–May	4 in (10 cm)
M. neglectum	black/pale blue	March–April	10 in (25 cm)
M. tubergenianum	dark blue, light blue tip	April–May	6 in (15 cm)

Narcissus (Liliaceae), narcissus

Narcissi will not develop and flower at their best until the second year. Plant several together or, if they are intended to naturalize, just scatter them widely, bulb by bulb.

More than 10,000 varieties are given in the "Classified List and International Register of Daffodil Names." The botanical narcissi are most appropriate for small gardens and rock gardens. Most of the others do well under deciduous tress, where the ground is still damp in the spring. The small-flowered and shorter species and varieties are suitable for containers. The hoop petticoat narcissus, *Narcissus bulbocodium* ssp *vulgaris* var. *conspicuus*, which bears the least resemblance to the other narcissi, is abbreviated in the list given below.

Botanical narcissi

Small narcissi are best in rock gardens and in pots. They are often too delicate for combinations with other plants.

The bluest grape hyacinth is Muscari azureum.

The pheasant's eye narcissus is one of the best naturalizing bulbs for a wild garden.

N. caniculatus	white, small yellow cup		4 in (10 cm)
N. minor	yellow	March	2 in (5 cm)
N. nanus (N.lobularis)	yellow	March	8 in (20 cm)
N. odorus	bright yellow	April–May	12 in (30 cm)
N. o. 'Plenus'	bright yellow, double	April–May	12 in (30 cm)

Poet's narcissi (poeticus narcissi)

These are among the most fragrant narcissi. The naturalizing narcissi, 'Pheasant's Eye', 'Keats' and 'Actaea', are single, long-stemmed, silvery-white and have a very small cup. They are also suitable for long grass. They outdo all other narcissi that are recommended for naturalizing, even though they propagate slowly. Give them a helping hand by spacing the bulbs a little farther apart from each other when you plant them.

N. poeticus var. *recurvus* 'Pheasant's Eye'		16 in (40 cm)
N. p. 'Actaea'	white, yellow cup orange edge	16 in (40 cm)
N. p. 'Keats'	delicate white, yellow cup, orange edge	16 in (40 cm)
N. p. 'Sinopel'	white, green cup, yellow edge	16 in (40 cm)

Trumpet narcissi

The trumpet of the well-known tall, fairly late narcissus is just as long as or even longer than its petals. Use this bulb with care, though, as in the very small garden, the large flowers ruin any sense of proportion.

Narcissus *'Ice Follies'*.

N. 'Golden Harvest'	yellow	22 in (55 cm)
N. 'King Alfred'	yellow	20 in (50 cm)
N. 'Mount Hood'	cream	22 in (55 cm)

Large-cupped narcissi

These often-planted narcissi are also less suitable for small gardens. The cup of this narcissus is always shorter than the petals.

N. 'Carlton'	yellow	18 in (45 cm)
N. 'Flower Record'	white, dark yellow cup	18 in (45 cm)
N. 'Fortune'	golden yellow, orange-red cup	18 in (45 cm)
N. 'Ice Follies'	light yellow, bright yellow cup	16 in (40 cm)
N. 'Prof Einstein'	white, bright orange cup	16 in (40 cm)

Small-cupped narcissi

Short or small-cupped narcissi are suitable for naturalization and give the best cut flowers. They flower late.

N. 'Barrett Browning'	white, orange cup	18 in (45 cm)
N. 'Quirinus'	lemon yellow, yellowy-orange cup	20 in (50 cm)
N. 'Verger'	white, dark red cup	16 in (40 cm)

Double narcissi

In sheltered sites this comparatively heavy flower does not get blown down. These narcissi, which give an old-fashioned effect, are suitable for planting in flower beds, but also in the border. They have no recognizable cup, as this has changed into some petals.

N. 'Dick Wilden'	yellow	16 in (40 cm)
N. 'Flower Drift'	creamy white, orange-red cup	14 in (35 cm)
N. 'Ice King'	white, creamy yellow cup	16 in (40 cm)
N. 'Petit Four'	white/apricot (only double-cupped)	14 in (35 cm)
N. 'Texas'	yellow/orange	14 in (35 cm)
N. 'White Lion'	white/soft yellow	16 in (40 cm)

Split-cupped narcissi (orchid narcissi) The cup of these medium-height narcissi is split and rather frilly. They are also sometimes called orchid-flowered narcissi because of their peculiar flower shape. They flower reasonably early.

N. 'Canasta'	white, yellow cup	6 in (15 cm)
N. 'Colblanc'	ivory white	16 in (40 cm)
N. 'Dolly Mollinger'	ivory white, cream/orange cup	18 in (45 cm)
N. 'Marie José'	cream, yellow star in cup	12 in (30 cm)
N. 'Orangerie'	silver white, orange cup	16 in (40 cm)
N. 'Parisienne'	silver white, dark orange cup	16 in (40 cm)
N. 'Printal'	cream, soft-yellow feathery cup	

Cyclamen-flowered narcissi The rock garden narcissus flowers exceptionally early, often with several flowers per stem. It can be recognized by the reflexed petals and long cup.

Narcissus *'Dick Wilden'.*

Narcissus *'February Gold'*.

N. 'February Gold'	yellow	10 in (25 cm)
N. 'February Silver'	creamy white	10 in (25 cm)
N. 'Dove Wings'	white, yellow cup	
N. 'Jack Snipe'	white, yellow cup	8 in (20 cm)
N. 'Jetfire'	yellow, orange cup	10 in (25 cm)
N. 'Peeping Tom'	deep yellow	14 in (35 cm)
N. 'Tête-à-Tête'	yellow, darker small cup	8 in (20 cm)

Jonquils (strongly scented)

Jonquils, the most heavily scented narcissi, prefer not to be in shade. They are extremely well suited for containers, even for indoors. They have small cups.

N. 'Baby Moon'	soft yellow	10 in (25 cm)
N. 'Bellsong'	yellow, pink cup	12 in (30 cm)
N. 'Buffawn'	orange-brown, pale orange cup	16 in (40 cm)
N. 'Dicksissel'	greeny yellow	12 in (30 cm)
N. 'Sundial'	dark yellow, green center	10 in (25 cm)

Tazetta narcissi

These scented narcissi have whole bunches of small-cupped flowers on one stem.

N. 'Cheerfulness'	white, double, orange center	20 in (50 cm)
N. 'Cragford'	white, orange cup	16 in (40 in)
N. 'Geranium'	white, orange cup	16 in (40 in)

N. 'Minnow'	pale yellow, sulfur-yellow cup		12 in (30 cm)
N. 'Yellow Cheerfulness'	soft yellow, double		20 in (50 cm)

Narcissus *'Thalia'.*

***Narcissus triandus,* angel's tears narcissus**

These very low-growing, late narcissi have several small, nodding, fragrant flowers on each stem. They are very graceful as the petals sweep back.

N. triandus var. *albus*	cream	April	6 in (15 cm)
N. 'Hawera'	bright yellow	April–May	8 in (20 cm)
N. 'Liberty Bells'	soft yellow	May	14 in (35 cm)
N. 'Petrel'	silvery white		8 in (20 cmn)
N. 'Shot Silk'	silvery white		14 in (35 cm)
N. 'Silver Chimes'	white, cream cup		12 in (30 cm)
N. 'Thalia'	silvery white	April–May	14 in (35 cm)
N. 'White Marvel'	true white, double		14 in (35 cm)

Miniature narcissi

Various small, low-growing narcissi each has its own flower shape. *N. bulbocodium* ssp *vulgaris* var. *conspicuus* needs a sunny site on ground that is not too dry.

N. asturiensis	yellow	Feb.	3 in (8 cm)
N. bulbocodium	yellow, large cup, small petals		6 in (15 cm)
N. 'W.P. Milner'	sulfur-yellow	April	8 in (20 cm)
N. 'Minnow'	white, yellow cup, multi-flowered	April	8 in (20 cm)
N. pseudonarcissus 'Lobularis'	white, yellow cup	Feb.	6 in (15 cm)
N. p. ssp *obvallaris*	golden yellow	Feb.–March	12 in (30 cm)
N. 'Rip van Winkle'	bright yellow, double	April	12 in (30 cm)
N. 'Topolino'	sulfur-yellow, canary yellow cup		6 in (15 cm)

***Nectarascordum* (Liliaceae)**

It is not just the special flower, but also the seed capsules which are attractive. Put them in a warm site in good, well-drained soil. This plant used to be called *Allium bulgaricum*, as well as *A. dioscorides* and *A. siculum*, as it looks like the allium.

N. siculum	green and purple, white edge	June	20 in (50 cm)

***Notholirion* (Liliaceae)**

This plant needs soil with a high organic content, but well-drained, because of its sensitivity to frost. Plant it between small shrubs, for example, to protect it from the east wind.

N. campanulatum	pinky purple	May–June	3 ft (1 m)
N. hyacinthinum	pale purple	June–July	3 ft (1 m)
N. thomsonianum	soft violet	April–May	5 ft (1.5 m)

Nectarascordum siliculum *gives an untidy effect. Plant as ornamental onions on dry, lime-rich sunny soil.*

Ornithogalum (Liliaceae), star of Bethlehem

With the exception of *O. umbellatum* and *O. balansae*, these bulbs, which naturalize well, are good cut flowers. The chincherinchee, *O. thyrsoides*, a tender species from South Africa, is often found at the florist's. The orange-colored *O. dubium* is also tender. *O. nutans*, the nodding star of Bethlehem, will also grow in shade. Like *O. umbellatum*, this bulb can spread, even too invasively.

O. arabicum	white	May-June	24 in (60 cm)
O. balansae	white/green	March–April	6 in (15 cm)
O. dubium	orange	April–May	12 in (30 cm)
O. magnum	white	May–June	24 in (60 cm)
O. narbonense	white	April–May	12 in (30 cm)
O. nutans	white/silvery-green	April	12 in (30 cm)
O. pyramidale	white	June	4 ft (1.2 m)
O. sintenisii	white, green stripe	April	4 in (10 cm)
O. umbellatum	white	April	6 in (15 cm)

When you see the "hairy" bulbs of the oxalis, you won't believe that they can produce such a beauty. There is no visible top or bottom to the bulbs so just plant them as they come!

Oxalis (Oxalidaceae)

The hardy, free-flowering rock plant *O. adenophylla* is native to South America. Plant it in a site which is not too damp in order to prevent rotting in winter. It might be sensible to cover it with a plate of glass. *O. deppei* (lucky clover) is not hardy, but it is often available in spring as a house plant. The other species are also suitable for a frost-free cold greenhouse.

O. adenophylla	pink	summer	8 in (20 cm)

Puschkinia (Liliaceae)

It can be difficult to tell *Puschkinia* apart from the low-growing *Scilla* and *Chionodoxa*, with the same growing conditions.

P. scilloides var. *libanotica*	china blue	March	8 in (20 cm)
P. s. var. *L.* 'Alba'	silver white	March	8 in (20 cm)

Ranunculus (Ranunculaceae), pilewort

These are hard to get going, but even harder to get rid of. Particularly on clay soil, this plant can become a nuisance. Various strains with copper-colored foliage and pale yellow or white flowers are in cultivation. In damp conditions on clay soil, the plant can easily grow to 16 in (40 cm) high and crowd out all the permanent plants coming up. Even in April, it can totally cover the ground in green, but in June the plant will already have died back again. It can be propagated by means of small rhizomes, but also by means of small bulbils in the leaf axils. Only people with natural gardens on sandy soil should grow this plant. They will be less rampant on poor soil.

R. ficaria	yellow	March–April	4 in (10 cm)
R. f. 'Alba'	cream	March–April	4 in (10 cm)
R. f. 'Flore Pleno'	yellow, double	March–April	4 in (10 cm)

Sanguinaria (Papaveraceae), bloodroot

The sap in this plant is bright red throughout, but especially in the roots. Do not let the delicate rhizomes dry out before planting. Even after planting, these North American forest plants require moisture-

This bulb, which is still often known as Puschkinia libanotica, *spreads freely on light clay soils.*

These Scilla sibirica *are one of the best naturalizing bulbs for a reasonably damp lawn. If the drainage channel is dredged regularly, the silt can be used as a good growing medium for this bulb.*

retentive, well-drained peaty soil in partial shade. A cool site is best.

S. canadensis	white	May–June	15cm (6in)
S. c. 'Plena'	white, double		15cm (6in)

Scilla (Liliaceae), Siberian squill

A number of species which used to come under the *Scilla* genus are now classified under the *Hyacinthoides* genus. The species names given below have already changed many times. Just to make it complicated, the family name has changed from Hyacinthaceae to Liliaceae. It is impracticable to name all the synonyms. They should be planted preferably in moisture-retentive lime-rich sand and clay soils with a low humus content. *S. peruviana* is not hardy. *S. sibirica* (Siberian squill) can be considered as one of the best naturalizing bulbs. Due to its early growing cycle, the grass can be mown reasonably on time. *S. autumnalis* (see Fall-flowering bulbous and tuberous plants), *S. greilhuberi,* and *S. peruviana* are more expensive species. Provide winter protection.

S. bifolia	gentian-blue	March	4 in (10 cm)
S. b. 'Rosea'	pinkish	March	4 in (10 cm)
S. greilhuberi	violet-blue	March–April	12 in (30 cm)
S. ingridae var.*taurica*	bright blue	March	6 in (15 cm)
S. litardieri	pastel mauve to lavender blue	May–June	6 in (15 cm)
S. mischtschenkoana	very pale blue	Feb.–March	4 in (10 cm)

Scilla sibirica *'Spring Beauty' has rather larger flowers than the common species.*

S. peruviana	bright blue	April–June	12 in (30 cm)
S. sibirica	bright blue	March–April	4 in (10 cm)
S. s. 'Alba'	white	March–April	4 in (10 cm)
S. s. 'Spring Beauty'	dark blue	March–April	4 in (10 cm)
S. tubergeniana	china blue with white	Feb.–March	3 in (8 cm)

***Trillium* (Liliaceae)**

The best species with rhizomatous roots come from woodland areas in the United States and Canada and are more suitable for garden use than the Asiatic species. They are easy to recognize from the three small petals at the top of a bare stem, which again also has three small leaves.

Of the fifty different species, most look very similar and are rather slow growers. Plant them in humus-rich soil in partial shade.

T. cernuum	white/pinkish	April-May	16 in (40 cm)
T. erectum	deep purple/green	April–May	
T. grandiflorum	white, large	April–May	12 in (30 cm)
T. nivale	white	April–May	6 in (15 cm)
T. sessile	browny-green	May–June	8 in (20 cm)
T. s. 'Luteum'	yellow	April–May	6 in (15 cm)
T. undulatum	white/red, variegated leaf		4 in (10 cm)

Triteleia (Liliaceae) The flower appears after the dying foliage in this bulbous plant, which resembles *Brodiaea*, a name also often used by growers. The foliage is unprepossessing, so put it in a sunny site between other plants, ground-cover plants, for example. Some winter protection is advisable in very cold areas. *T. laxa* with onion-like flowers is the best known.

T. ixioides 'Splendens'	yellow, dark stripes	June	20 in (50 cm)
T. hendersonii	yellow	June–July	12 in (30 cm)
T. laxa 'Koningin Fabiola'	violet-purple	June	20 in (50 cm)

This bulb is still on the market under the name of Brodiaea *'Koningin Fabiola'. Perhaps the fault lies with me, but I have never been able to take such a pretty photo in my own garden.*

Tulipa (Liliaceae), tulip Striped tulips are once again in fashion. In the old tulip varieties, a virus gave rise to the phenomenon of "broken," "bizarre," or "fine," which is how the variegated colors in the tulip were thought of. The most-diseased tulips were the most expensive. The frantic speculation in tulips was the result. The *Tulipa* 'Queen of Night' is still considered to be the blackest tulip, but the parrot tulip 'Black Parrot' is not far behind. The tulip is subdivided into different groups – for characteristics, see below.

This is a practical classification for growers. A botanically correct classification according to origin would look completely different. The different groups are shown below in order of flowering period.

Duc van Tol tulips These are the earliest-flowering tulips. The small flowers have tapering petals.

Single early tulips These are suitable for growing indoors and for planting in flower beds. They flower in mid-April with an average height of 10 in (25 cm). The 'Brilliant Star' is often sold as the 'Christmas tulip'.

Double early tulips These plump-bloomed tulips flower in mid-April and are suitable for bowls and flower beds.

Mendel tulips Mendel tulips were developed at the beginning of this century by crossing 'Duc van Tol' tulips with Darwin tulips. They flower after the middle of April. They are cultivated as cut flowers and are suitable for various purposes in the garden.

Triumph tulips Crosses between early and late tulips resulted in this group. They flower at the end of April.

Darwin tulips These tulips are the most frequently grown tulips, both for picking and for the garden.

Darwin hybrids Crosses between the Darwins and different varieties of *Tulipa fosteriana* resulted in this group, suitable as a cut flower. The shiny petals are striking. The 'Apeldoorn' variety is the most widely known.

Tulipa acuminata *from Turkey with its small petals has a green flush on the outside.*

Breeder tulips The flowering period for this group is the same as for the one above. The flowers do not have the gloss of the Darwin hybrids, but apart from that they are just as good to use.

Lily-flowered tulips The pointed petals thrust outwards somewhat at the top. All varieties are single-flowered and late-flowering.

Cottage tulips Crosses were made with late-flowering single-flowered tulips which were said to have been found in old English gardens.

Rembrandt tulips These Darwin tulips with striped or speckled flowers have become very popular again in the past few years. The flamed flowers often come about due to a viral infection. In the seventeenth century it was thought that the color transferred from one bulb to another if two bulbs were cut in half and placed next to each other. In fact, it was the virus that transferred from one bulb to the other. These viruses also reduce growing strength and thus bulb growth.

Parrot tulips Parrot tulips have deeply incised flowers with crenated and fringed edges that open very wide. They have arisen from "sports" of various tulips from a number of groups.

Peony-flowered

These tulips, also called double late tulips, are not widely grown.

Multi-flowered

This separate group of tulips has several flowers on one stem.

T. 'Georgette'	yellow, red edge	3–5 blooms	20 in (50 cm)
T. 'Toronto'	bright pink	2–3 blooms	12 in (30 cm)
T. 'Wallflower'	purple-brown	4–6 blooms	20 in (50 cm)
T. orphanidea 'Flava'	yellow, red tips	April–May	8 in (20 cm)
T. praestans: see botanical tulips			
T. pulchella 'Liliput'	red	April	4 in (10 cm)

Botanical species

The botanical species or species tulips are further subdivided into different groups by origin. The cultivated varieties of these groups are also called "botanical" for the sake of convenience. Most of them flower very early to early. The plants are very different in appearance. All these tulips can stay in the ground during the summer. Plant them in a site where the sun shines on the ground; in a warm, dry site, they reach the budding stage earlier and flower better. Botanical tulips are the best ones for the rock garden and the small town garden. They have been of increasing interest in the past few years, as have the old striped tulips. *Tulipa sylvestris* (wild tulip) can be planted in the grass, provided it is mown late. This bulbous plant belongs to the naturalized or "old stone ruin" plant group. Other tulips that are good for naturalization are *T. hageri*, *T. tarda*, *T. turkestanica*, and *T.*

Nearly all tulips, whether they are tall or short, bright or soft in color, show to their best advantage when they are planted close together in large groups.

Tulipa batalinii *is seldom grown. Crosses between* T. batalinii *and* T. linifolia *produced the varieties mentioned.*

wilsoniana. The *T. hoogiana*, *T. ingens*, *T. lanata*, and *T. sosnowskyi* species are expensive, which makes them special and exclusive.

T. acuminata	red/yellow	April	20 in (50 cm)
T. agenensis	brown-scarlet	April	8 in (20 cm)
T. albertii	orange scarlet	April	8–10 in (20–25 cm)
T. altaica	yellow/crimson red	April–May	12 in (30 cm)
T. aucherana	deep pink	April	2 in (5 cm)
T. aximensis	red, initial gray flush	May	14 in (35 cm)
T. bakeri	purple, yellow base	March–April	4 in (10 cm)
T. b. 'Lilac Wonder'	pale purple, dark yellow center	April	8 in (20 cm)
T. batalinii	yellow	April	6 in (15 cm)
T. b. 'Apricot Jewel'	orange-red	April	8 in (20 cm)
T. b. 'Bright Gem'	sulfur-yellow	April	8 in (20 cm)
T. b. 'Bronze Charm'	bronze/salmon color	May	4 in (10 cm)
T. b. 'Red Jewel'	bright red	April	6 in (15 cm)
T. b. 'Yellow Jewel'	yellow, pink	April	8 in (20 cmn)
T. biflora	white/green	April	6–10 in (15–25 cm)
T. carinata	red, crimson red flush	April	12 in (30 cm)
T. celsiana	red	May	4 in (10 cm)

Tulipa kolpakowskiana from China has wavy foliage and a crooked stem.

T. chrysantha	yellow	April	8 in (20 cm)
T. clusiana	white/red	April–May	12 in (30 cm)
T. c. 'Cynthia'	cream/red	April–May	12 in (30 cm)
T. dasystemon	yellow	May	6 in (15 cm)
T. eichleri	crimson red, yellow stripe	April	10 in (25 cm)
T. ferganica	yellow/pinkish	April	6 in (15 cm)
T. grengiolensis	soft yellow, red edge	April–May	12 in (30 cm)
T. hageri	red	April	6 in (15 cm)
T. h. 'Splendens'	bronze-colored	April	8 in (20 cm)
T. hoogiana	orange-red, dark center, yellow edge	April–May	18 in (45 cm)
T. humilis, see *T. pulchella*			
T. ingens	red, black specks on the base, red stem	April	16 in (40 in)
T. kolpakowskiana	yellow/greenish	April	6 in (15 cm)
T. kurdica	red to orange-red	May–June	8 in (20 cm)
T. lanata	orange-red, yellow edge	April	10 in (25 cm)
T. linifolia	scarlet red	April–May	6 in (15 cm)
T. marjolettii	soft yellow/pink edge	May	20 in (50 cm)
T. mauritiana	red, yellow base	end May	14 in (35 cm)

Tulipa praestans 'Fusilier', the most popular botanical tulip.

Tulipa pulchella var. humilis flowers very early. The flowers are sturdy – they will withstand a rain or hail shower.

T. m. 'Cindy'	yellow, red edge	May	14 in (35 cm)
T. maximowiczii	vivid red, black center	April–May	6 in (15 cm)
T. orphanidea	orange, dark center	April–May	8 in (20 cm)
T. ostrowskiana	orange-red, green, black with yellow center	April	10 in (25 cm)
T. passeriniana	red, dark purple center, cream edge	May	20 in (50 cm)
T. polychroma	white/yellow center	April	4 in (10 cm)
T. praestans	red	April	10 in (25 cm)
T. p. 'Fusilier'	vivid orange-red, multi-flowered	April	8 in (20 cm)
T. p. 'Tubergens Var.'	red, multi-flowered	April	10 in (25 cm)
T. p. 'Unicum'	orange-red	April	6–8 in (15–20 cm)
T. pulchella var. *humilis*	violet/pink	Feb.–March	4 in (10 cm)
T. p. var. *violacea*	bright purple-violet	Feb.–March	4 in (10 cm)
T. p. 'Liliput'	red	April	4 in (10 cm)
T. p. 'Zephyr'	orange-red, yellow center	April	8 in (20 cm)
T. saxatilis	pink-purply-pink	Mar.–April	12 in (30 cm)
T. schrenkii	red, orange edge	April	4 in (10 cm)
T. sylvestris	yellow	April	10 in (25 cm)
T. tarda	yellow/white	April	4 in (10 cm)
T. tetraphylla	yellow, outside purple specks	May	8 in (20 cm)
T. tubergeniana	scarlet	April	16-20 in (40-50 cm)
T. t. 'Splendens'	vivid scarlet red	April	16-20 in (40-50 cm)
T. turkestanica	white, yellow heart	March	10 in (25 cm)
T. urumiensis	golden yellow, red stripes	April–May	8 in (20 cm)
T. whittallii	bronze-colored, orange-yellow	April	10 in (25 cm)
T. wilsoniana	vermilion red	May	4 in (10 cm)

Other tulips

T. greigii, *T. fosteriana*, and *T. kaufmanniana* and their hybrids are not counted as "botanical" tulips; crosses between them make their extraction unclear. With regard to tulip hybrids, I refer the reader to the most recent growers' catalogs; it is pointless to mention the range of thousands of varieties, which changes each year. I will make an exception for the three species mentioned above, as they are quite suitable for the small garden, both for separate flower beds and for borders and containers. For a number of varieties of *T. kaufmanniana*, the striped foliage is an extra attraction.

T. greigii hybrids

T. 'Red Riding Hood'	bright scarlet red, black center	8 in (20 cm)

Tulipa turkestanica comes from North West China and, as the name suggests, from Turkestan. It is one of the earliest-flowering tulips.

Tulipa urumiensis from Iran opens its flowers wide in the sun.

T. 'Plaisir	creamy white with vivid red stripes	8 in (20 cm)
T. 'Sparkling Fire'	vermilion red	8 in (20 cm)
T. fosteriana hybrids		
T. 'Mme Lefèbre', see *T.* 'Red Emperor'		
T. 'Red Emperor'	scarlet red, large	14 in (35 cm)
T. 'White Emperor'	silver white, yellow heart	20 in (50 cm)
T. kaufmanniana hybrids		
T. 'Concerto'	brilliant white, slightly yellow	8 in (20 cm)
T. 'Heart's Delight'	crimson red, pale pink edge	10 in (25 cm)
T. 'Johann Strauss'	red, white edge, inside white, yellow center	8 in (20 cm)
T. 'Showwinner'	deep red, yellow center	8 in (20 cm)

Uvularia (Liliaceae)

This good hardy rhizomatous plant native to North America requires the same conditions as the European Solomon's seal: soil with a high organic content and partial shade.

The plant is one of the latest spring-flowering plants and is suitable for naturalization in the slightly acid woodland garden. Sometimes the rhizomes are supplied loose in peat, but more often this plant is sold at nurseries as a permanent plant.

U. grandiflora	lemon yellow	May–June	20 in (50 cm)
U. sessilifolia	yellowy green		8 in (20 cm)

Summer-Flowering Bulbous and Tuberous Plants

It is sometimes difficult to differentiate between summer-flowering bulbous plants for the garden and those for indoors. Most require a cool room or a warm garden.

Acidanthera *is also grown as a cut flower.*

It is not always possible to meet both requirements. Most of these plants have to be lifted in the fall to overwinter in a cool or warm place indoors. It depends on the species whether they have to be lifted as early as September or if they can wait until November. In frost-free regions they can be left out in the garden.

Of the rhizomatous plants, some are supplied as loose rhizomes, for example the trumpet flower (*Incarvillea*); others are treated and sold as permanent plants. For this reason, plants such as the Peruvian lily (*Alstroemeria*) and Solomon's seal (*Polygonatum*) are not discussed in this book.

It is a pity that in the case of summer bulbs people often think only of gladioli, begonias, and dahlias. Even lilies do not spring to mind straight away. Vivid color contrasts can be made with summer bulbs, but they can also mix in harmoniously in a border. There are not many permanent plants for a red or orange border, but it is exactly in the bulbous and tuberous plants that many of these colors are to be found, as well as the variation which is so badly needed in these borders.

People who as a rule do not want to spend much time on their garden are better advised to concern themselves with spring- and fall-flowering bulbous plants: that means planting them just once and then enjoying them for years. A lot of work has to be put in to produce the best results with summer-flowering plants: planting, mulching, lifting, and protecting the plants. The plants in this chapter are essential for the flowery and colorful summer garden. Wafts of scent would go well with this sea of flowers, but unfortunately bulbous plants do not excel in the scent department. Some lilies (*Lilium auratum, L. candidum*, and *L. regale*), *Acidanthera*, and *Galtonia* are the only exceptions.

Nearly all summer-flowering bulbs need absolutely full sun. Thus in gardens with a lot of trees it is better to use spring-and fall-flowering bulbs. With spring bulbs, the usual colors are yellow, blue, and white; the summer-flowering bulbs shine out in yellow, orange, and red. Real blue is hardly ever found in the summer-flowering plants.

Following page:
Anemone *'Syphide'*

***Acidanthera* (Iridaceae)**

Plant them in May and lift the corms when they have produced offsets in October-November.

Give them a warm sunny site. They are also suitable for (large) flowerpots.

A. bicolor	creamy, purple specks	August	32 in (80 cm)
A. tubergenii	white, dark center	July	32 in (80 cm)

Aconitum (Ranunculaceae), climbing monkshood

This tuberous plant from the subalpine regions of Mongolia, among other places, needs support. Let the soft, weak stems grow through a low-growing shrub – this shrub will then appear to flower twice. There is usually only one flower at the end of the stem, of the same shape as the permanent monkshood plant. It is cultivated from seed and grows

Really, there is nothing quite like a blue agapanthus, but this plant also has much to offer the white garden.

in sun and partial shade. It definitely requires some winter protection.

A. volubile	blue	July–Aug.	4 ft (1.2 m)

***Agapanthus* (Liliaceae), African lily**

The most old-fashioned plant for tubs is still one of the best. Sometimes, however, it does not want to flower. Leave it to overwinter in a cool, but frost-free site and put it in a well-drained pot that is not too big. They have good and bad years – one year they will flower better than the next. They seem to flower less well when they have overwintered in warm conditions. They do not need much light. From the second half of May (not too early), they can go outside in a warm sunny spot; give them plenty of water then. I prefer to see the agapanthus only as a tub plant, but if you have a warm site which is fairly dry in winter, this bulbous plant can also be used as a garden plant. Don't forget to cover it well with compost or leaf mold when there is a frost.

A. africanus	blue		3 ft (1 m)
A. a. 'Albidus'	white	Aug.–Sept.	28 in (70 cm)
A. (hybr. cult.) 'Blue Triumphater'	blue	Aug.–Sept.	32 in (80 cm)
A. 'Donau'	blue	July–Aug.	4 ft (1.2 m)
A. 'Bright Blue'	bright blue		24 in (60 cm)
A. 'Isis'	blue, free-flowering		
A. 'Kingston Blue'	blue, large flower		
A. 'Liliput'	blue-purple	July–Aug.	18 in (45 cm)
A. 'Loch Hope'	dark blue		4 ft (1.2 m)
A. 'Peter Pan'	blue		12 in (30 cm)
A. orientalis	blue, smaller		20 in (50 cm)

***Allium* (Liliaceae), ornamental onion**

For the sake of convenience, all ornamental onions have been included under the spring-flowering bulbs. Some actually flower at the beginning of the summer at a time when permanent plants are already fully grown. This presents many opportunities for pretty combinations in the border. Pay close attention to the height of the alliums, so they are not hidden away between the flowers of the permanent plants when they flower.

The onions can be scattered singly over the border or planted in reasonably large groups, repeated in a few places.

***Amaryllis* (Liliaceae)**

This plant should not be confused with *Hippeastrum*, which is suitable only for growing indoors. The bulb can stay in the ground in a very sheltered, warm site with well-drained soil. Plant the bulbs a good 10 in (25 cm) deep and only in spring. However, the ground in a cold greenhouse, where the soil warms up in the summer, is more suitable. The plant can be propagated by seed as well as by using the bulbils.

The amaryllis comes from South Africa, which clarifies the difference from *Hippeastrum*: the latter comes from South America.

A. belladonna	pink	Aug.–Sept.	20 in (50 cm)

Allium rosenbachianum *'Album' is an example of a late-flowering ornamental onion. There are at least 100 star-shaped little flowers in a globe.*

***Begonia* (Begoniaceae), tuberous begonia**

There are more than 1,000 species and a few even tolerate frost, but most come under the indoor plant group. The bedding begonia is, of course, widely known. The begonias mentioned in this section have tubers. The garden plants are all derived from *Begonia tuberosa* and are essential in a cottage garden. They can also look splendid planted in Victorian flower beds.*

Treat tuberous begonias like dahlias. Don't plant them too early, as a late-night frost can do a lot of damage. If the plants have already come up when frost is still expected, earth them in again, so that the foliage is underground, or put upturned flowerpots over the plants. Lift them in mid-October and let them overwinter in a cool place in dry peat. It would be too difficult to name the constantly changing range of varieties; I therefore list the various groups below.

Large-flowered hybrids, the grandifloras, belong to the largest group. These were the first to come onto the market:

camellia-flowered	crenated flowers
rose-flowered	marbled flowers
frilly flowers	striped flowers

Multiflora Maxima hybrids are free-flowering medium-sized tuberous begonias about 10 in (25 cm) high.

The tuberous begonias are best for large drifts of color in the summer. The beds can be planted with pansies in the early spring.

Small-flowered hybrids, the multifloras, are medium-sized and more tender than the large-flowered members of their species.

B. 'Bertinii'	orange, pendent

Weeping begonias, the Flore-pleno pendulas, have relatively small flowers and soft, pendulous stems.

***Bryonia* (Cucurbitaceae), white bryony**

This poisonous plant which is considered to be indigenous has a tuberous rhizome in the ground that can become quite large. In the wild, they are found in woods and dunes. It is a dioecious plant, i.e., male and female flowers are on different plants, and it needs lime-rich soil. This plant makes me wonder why indigenous plants are so rarely sold. Like the spring-flowering *Gagea,* it is a climbing plant that is valuable for garden use.

B. cretica subsp. *dioica*	June–Aug.	6–13 ft (2–4 m)

***Canna* (Cannaceae), Indian shot**

The well-known canna, which gives a garden such a tropical feel, is easy to keep only if it can overwinter in a warm place (at least 60°F [15°C]). Split the rhizomes in the spring and clean them (remove rotten parts). Put them in a warm place from mid-March. They can be placed outside from mid-May, either planted out in the garden or in a large pot on the patio. Even just one pot of cannas can make its mark in a patch of the garden where not much is flowering.

The *Canna indica* hybrids were particularly popular in the last century. These hybrids were produced from crosses between four species. No fewer than a thousand varieties were cultivated, but most of them have disappeared again.

C. generalis 'Wyoming'	orange to bronze-colored brown foliage	4 ft (1.2 m)
C. hybr. 'America'	vivid scarlet red, brown foliage	3 ft (1 m)
C. h. 'Brilliant'	red, green foliage	3 ft (1 m)
C. h. 'Golden Lucifer'	silver yellow, green foliage	24 in (60 cm)
C. h. 'Lucifer'	bright red, yellow edge, green foliage	24 in (60 cm)
C. h. 'President'	scarlet red, green foliage	36 in (90 cm)
C. h. 'Salmon Pink'	pink, green foliage	32 in (80 cm)
C. malawiensis 'Variegata'	foliage with yellowy-green veins	

Chlidanthus (Liliaceae)

This rarely seen bulbous plant originates from South America. Plant it outside in a very warm site, not before mid-May. As with the canna, let it overwinter in a warm place. They are also suitable for room cultivation. The chlidanthus is an example of a monotypical genus, a plant genus of which only one species is known.

C. fragrans	bright yellow	June–July	10 in (25 cm)

The canna is native over tropical and subtropical areas throughout the world. In many areas they have also naturalized.

Commelina
(Commelinaceae)

This is not really a bulbous or tuberous plant, but the fleshy rhizome can be stored well. It is closely related to the tradescantia, a well-known indoor and permanent garden plant. Plant in spring and lift in October. Give it well-drained soil on a sunny site. Each flower opens separately, but for only a short time. It can multiply vigorously, but in view of its sensitivity to frost, it will never become invasive.

C. tuberosa (Coelestis group)	bright blue	June–Aug.	12 in (30 cm)
C. t. 'Alba'	white	June–Aug.	12 in (30 cm)

Crinum
(Amaryllidaceae)

The rich soil in a cold greenhouse is suitable, but, with good protection, it can overwinter outside. In that case, give it a very sheltered site and well-drained soil. Plant them 16 in (40 cm) apart and leave the nose of the long bulb above ground. In cultivation, there is only *C.* x *powellii*, a cross between the *C. moorei* and *C. bulbispermum* species, both from South Africa.

C. x *powellii*	pink	Aug.–Sept.	3 ft (1 m)
C. p. 'Album'	white	Aug.–Sept.	3 ft (1 m)

Crinum x powellii.

Crocosmia masonorum is the most common, but not the prettiest due to its rather indeterminate color.

Crocosmia* (Iridaceae), *montbretia

The plant resembles the freesia, but grows taller and is therefore more suitable as a cut flower. Some species are frost-hardy, but even then winter protection is still advisable. Plant new corms from the end of March in well-drained soil. They can stay in the same site for a number of years. Propagate the crocosmia by planting out the cormlets.

C. masonorum	orange	August	3 ft (1 m)
C. x *crocosmiiflora* 'Aurora'	orange		28–36 in (70–90 cm)
C. x *c.* 'Carmen Brilliant'	crimson red, small-flowered		
C. x *c.* 'Citronella'	lemon yellow, small-flowered		
C. x *c.* 'His Majesty'	orange-yellow, crimson-red specks		
C. x *c.*'Lady Wilson'	orange		
C. x *c.* 'Lucifer'	red, reasonably winter-hardy		

***Cypella* (Iridaceae)**

Full sun and moisture-retentive soil are absolutely essential for this iris-like plant from South America (Argentina and Uruguay). Store the large round tubers in slightly moist peat dust over winter or protect them well in the garden in a sheltered site.

The other species of this genus are not suitable for northern climates, and are not commercially available.

C. herbertii	yellow/brown	June–Sept.	24 in (60 cm)

***Dahlia* (Asteraceae)**

Dahlias are usually sold in packs. When buying them, do not pay attention only to the pretty colored picture, but look closely at the contents: the size of the tubers varies quite a lot. Plant dahlias at the same time as potatoes, from May 1. If the plants have come up when there is still frost at night, put upturned flowerpots over them. They can be cut down and lifted in November. Store them in a cool, frost-free place. Do not let the tubers dry out; lay them in a box with dry sand or peat, but do not water them, as this can result in rotting.

Removing the top pair of side buds (this is called "disbudding") produces a large bloom on a straight stem. Dahlias need a good mulching. Mignon and miniature dahlias should be sown on a warm site in early spring. By fall they already will have produced small tubers, which can be lifted in October. These tubers do not have any eyes that can sprout, so that part of the stem where these eyes are situated must always stay on the tuber. For this reason, never pull the loose tubers out by the stem! Careful attention must also be paid to this when dividing a larger plant. There are a great number of varieties; I list here those generally available.

Topmix dahlia.

Anemone-flowered dahlia (height 12–16 in [30–40 cm])

These low and free-flowering dahlias with semi-double blooms are suitable for planting as edging, in containers and flower beds. The flowers are double:

D. 'Brio'	orange
D. 'Fabel'	red
D. 'Gamelan'	yellow
D. 'Honey'	faded pink with yellow center
D. 'Purpinka'	purple
D. 'Toto'	white

Orchid-flowered dahlia (height 32 in–3 ft [80 cm–1 m])

D. 'Giraffe'	orange
D. 'Pink Giraffe'	pink

Mignon dahlia (height 16-28 in [40–70 cm])

Single-flowered medium-height dahlias, suitable for flower beds and borders:

D. 'G.F. Hemerick'	orange
D. 'Firebird'	red
D. 'Roodkapje'	bright red
D. 'Mies'	mauve-pink
D. 'Sneezy'	white

'Red Riding Hood' mignon dahlia

Miniature dahlia or Topmix dahlia (12 in [30 cm])

These are early-flowering, low-growing, and single-flowered dahlias, suitable for containers and edging. They are usually sold not by name but by color and are easy to grow from seed.

Collarette dahlia (12-24 in [30–60 cm])

The single bloom has a circle of smaller petals around the center, the "collar." This collar is usually a different color:

D. 'Alstergruss'	dark orange, yellow collar

'Popular Guest' cactus dahlia.

	D. 'Hartenaas'	pink, white collar
	D. 'La Gioconda'	red with yellow collar

Cactus and semi-cactus dahlia (height 32 in–4 ft [80 cm–1.2 m])

These tall, relatively late double dahlias have fancy petals:

D. 'Bach'	vivid yellow
D. 'Bergers Record'	red
D. 'Collar Spectacle'	orange and white
D. 'Goldcrown'	orange
D. 'My Love'	white
D. 'Preference'	yellow
D. 'Firebird'	yellow and red
D. 'Red Majorette'	deep red, good cut flower

Cactus dahlia, pinwheel type

The petals are even more fancy than the above and curled. This gives the bloom a whirling appearance.

D. 'Jane'	mauve-purple
D. 'Popular Guest'	pale pinky-purple
D. 'Star's Elite'	salmon-pink with yellow center
D. 'White Star'	white
D. 'Yellow Star'	soft yellow

Decorative dahlia (height 32 in–4 ft [80 cm–1.2 m]) These include the most old-fashioned tall double dahlias with broad petals. They are easy and robust. This group includes an almost infinitely large number of varieties. Due to the frequently changing range, it is pointless to mention any of them.

Pompon dahlia (height 3–6 ft [1–2 m]) These are the longest-flowering dahlias. The round, compact bloom has long stems, suitable for picking.

D. 'White Aster'	white	3 ft (1 m)
D. 'Blomfontein'	purple-mauve, white tip	32 in (80 cm)

Ball dahlias The ball-shaped blooms of these fine dahlias are bigger than those of the pompon dahlias, but smaller than those of the decorative dahlias.

D. 'Eveline'	white, pink flush	32 in (80 cm)

You can put dahlias all over the place: every color can be found in each group for a specific height. I prefer a tranquil garden: only red or white and then using different heights, for example. No other plant is so easy to use as the dahlia for gardening "by colors."

Water lily dahlia (height 28 in–3 ft [70 cm–1 m]) Selecting from the small-flowered decorative dahlias produced this group. The bloom looks flattish. They are often supplied mixed.

Dahlias for flower-beds These dahlias are smaller and grow in a more compact way than the others.

D. 'Alstergruss'	orange/yellow
D. 'Ellen Houston'	(decorative) garnet red, brown foliage
D. 'Fascination'	(peony-flowered) mauve, brown foliage
D. 'Hartenaas'	(collarette) mauve-pink, lighter collar

Mixed freesias.

D. 'Little Tiger'	(decorative) red/white
D. 'Ludwig Helfert'	(cactus) orange
D. 'Park Princess'	(cactus) pink
D. 'Playa Blanca'	(cactus) white
D. 'Suzette'	(decorative) creamy yellow

Eucomis **(Liliaceae), pineapple flower** The cluster of flowers with a tuft of foliage on top brings to mind the fruit of a pineapple. The large bulbs, native to South Africa, can often be bought in the market in spring. They are suitable for planting out in the garden in the summer (after mid-May), but they are also easy tub plants, with an interesting shape. Due to its dark browny-green coloring, the pineapple flower has not become popular. It propagates by seed and after three years a plant capable of flowering is produced. It overwinters in a cool place, but not under 46°F (8°C). I would dispute the recommendation to leave the plants outside in the winter under a thick covering.

E. autumnalis	brilliant white	August	12 in (30 cm)
E. bicolor	purple-edged	August	20 in (50 cm)
E. b. 'Alba'	grubby white	August	20 in (50 cm)
E. comosus	white, mauve center	August	20 in (50 cm)

Freesia **(Iridaceae)** Although they can do better in the greenhouse, some are suitable for the garden. Store them at 70°F (20°C), then 86°F (30°C) for the last few months. It is almost impossible to meet these demands oneself, so it is best to buy fresh ones each year. In the spring, growers supply prepared corms that flower in August-September. They will be successful only in a beautiful summer on a moisture-retentive, sunny and warm site. Unfortunately they are nearly always supplied for the garden in single or double mixes.

Galtonia candidans, *a must for a big pot, but it can also go in a warm site in the garden.*

***Galtonia* (Liliaceae), summer hyacinth**

White, bell-shaped flowers hang from a long stem. They are not cold-hardy, but are suitable as a tub plant. Let them overwinter in a cool, dark place indoors.

Plant them in April and lift them again in October. The galtonia can remain outside only in warm sites with well-drained soil if good winter protection is used.

G. candidans	white	July–Aug.	5 ft (1.5 m)
G. viridiflora	white with green, pendulous bells	Aug.–Sept.	28 cm (70 cm)

x *Gladanthera* (Iridaceae)

This unusual plant is a cross between the gladiolus and the acidanthera. Such crosses are known as bigeneric hybrids. The flowers resemble those of the gladiolus; the scent is that of the acidanthera. It is a botanical rarity produced in New Zealand in 1955.

***Gladiolus* (Iridaceae)**

The large-flowered cut flower gladiolus is generally well known. The corms must be lifted each year and they are treated in exactly the same way as the dahlia. They are not usually supplied by the name of the variety, but "by color" or mixed. They need support and full sun.

The less well-known, smaller, more-or-less hardy, wild gladioli are suitable for permanent planting in the garden. These gladioli are native to South Africa, the Mediterranean area, and Central Europe. The botanical species can stay in the ground. These more refined species go well in a border. Innumerable varieties are classified in a number of groups: dwarf, miniature, small-flowered, medium large-flowered, large-flowered, very large-flowered.

Gladiolus *'Camborne'.*

Botanical species:

G. carneus	white/soft pinky-purple	April–May	24 in (60 cm)
G. communis	pinky-violet/red	May–June	20 in (50 cm)
G. imbricatus	deep purple	June–July	30 in (75 cm)
G. italicus	crimson red	June	32 cm (80 cm)

Large-flowered:

G. 'Camborne'	purple-pink, dark center
G. 'Cordula'	pillar-box red
G. 'Groene Specht'	yellowy-green
G. 'Friendship'	flesh-colored-pink
G. 'Invitation'	orchid-pinky-purple

Gladiolus *'Cordula'.*

Left: Gladiolus *'Leonore'.*

Right: Gloriosa rothschildiana. *The photo suggests that it is excessively free-flowering. Wouldn't it be much prettier to have a flower just here and there between shining green foliage?*

G. 'Leonore'	yellow
G. 'Memorial Day'	greeny-purple
G. 'My Love'	cream, pink frills
G. 'Sans Souci'	scarlet red
G. 'White Friendship'	silver white

***Gloriosa* (Liliaceae),** This plant is suitable only for people with a greenhouse. It can grow to 10 ft (3 m). Cut it down in fall and let it overwinter in a warm place. It is not a difficult plant, provided the temperature is always high enough.

It is often sold only as a room plant in the summer, always trained on a wire. It looks better using long canes to enable it to fulfil its climbing potential.

G. rothschildiana	yellow/red	July–Sept.	10 ft (3 m)

***Habranthus* (Liliaceae, Amaryllidaceae)** This plant is really suitable only for the cold greenhouse, but a warm site in a patio garden will also do. It likes full sun.

H. andersonii	coppery-yellow	July–Sept.	6 in (15 cm)

***Homeria* (Iridaceae)** This good, winter-hardy tuberous plant comes from South Africa. Both species with *Ixia*-like flowers are sometimes also supplied mixed. Plant them 2¾–3¼ in (7 to 8 cm) deep in late fall to avoid early growth and with it damage from night-frost in the spring.

The white trumpet flower is not often seen. It is usually sold in the spring as a permanent plant.

Winter protection is necessary. It has a long flowering period, but each bloom flowers separately for only one day.

H. flaccida can be found in most catalogs under the name of *H. collina* var. *aurantiaca*.

H. flaccida	orange	June–July	20 in (50 cm)
H. ochroleuca	yellow	June–July	28 in (70 cm)

Hymenocallis (Liliaceae)

Hymenocallis is best planted inside in pots in February to be put outside in the summer. It is also possible to plant them outside straight away into soil in a warm site in May. Bring them in again in October, when they need warmth.

The naming of this plant genus leads to great confusion. You still come across the names of *Elisena* and *Ismene*.

H. x *festalis*	white	June–July	24 in (60 cm)

Incarvillea (Bignoniaceae), trumpet flower

This plant likes a warm, sunny site that is not too moist because of frost sensitivity. It should be well-protected in winter. They can last for years only if planted in a good site, but it is better to pull them out of the ground in the fall and treat them as the dahlia. They are also suitable as a tub plant; they can stay in the pot in the winter. The low-growing *I. hybr.* 'Bees Pink' with beautiful large flowers is the most suitable one for pots.

Trumpet flower is often sold as a permanent plant, but the fleshy rhizomes can also sometimes be bought loose on the market. Keep the rhizome damp. They can be forced in the greenhouse for earlier flowering.

I. delavayi	pink	June	24 in (60 cm)
I. d. 'Alba'	white	June	24 in (60 cm)
I. hybr. 'Bees Pink'	pink	June	10 in (25 cm)

***Ixia* (Iridaceae)** Plant this ideal plant in well-drained, rich soils late, to prevent frost damage, and close together (ten in an area the size of a saucer), and give it plenty of winter protection. Lift it after flowering (except in the southwest where it can remain in the ground) and store the bulb in a warm place during the summer to imitate the dry South African summer. It might seem that this bulbous plant would be at its best as a cut flower in the greenhouse. Unfortunately, the bulbs are usually supplied mixed in gaudy red, pink, yellow, orange, and cream colors, all with a vivid darker center, which makes them unsuitable for people with refined gardens arranged by color. It can be propagated by planting out the corms and cormlets in the fall.

I. hybr. 'Blauwe Vogel'	white, black-purple center, striped outside		16 in (40 cm)
I. h. 'Giant'	cream, dark red center	June–Aug.	28 in (70 cm)
I. h. 'Hogarth'	cream, dark center		20 in (50 cm)
I. h. 'Mabel'	deep crimson pink	July	16 in (40 cm)

Ixia *'Hogarth' is one of the most frequently grown varieties.*

I. h. 'Rose Emperor'	soft pink, crimson red center	July	24 in (60 cm)
I. h. 'Titia'	fuchsia red, crimson red center		16 in (40 cm)
I. h. 'Uranus'	bright yellow, black center	July	20 in (50 cm)
I. paniculata	creamy-pink	Aug.–Sept.	16 in (40 cm)
I. speciosa	red	Aug.	20 in (50 cm)
I. viridiflora	green	June–July	20 in (50 cm)

Liatris *is often grown as a cut flower because of its sturdy stems.*

Lathyrus (Fabaceae)

Tubers grow in the second year on a winter-hardy rhizome. This plant probably came as a weed from Western Asia and is easy to grow from seed. The tubers can stay in the ground, but, once the seed is set, they can be allowed to overwinter in a cool place indoors. Propagate lathyrus by planting the (edible) tubers outside again.

L. tuberosus	pink	June–Sept.	4 ft (1.2 m)

Lapeirousia (Iridacea)

This small summer-flowering bulbous plant is suitable for the small garden or rock garden. Like most South African plants, it is not winter-hardy. Treat it more or less like freesia: plant in April and lift in October.

L. laxa	bright red, dark specks	July–Sept.	12 in (30 cm)

Lilium speciosum *'Rubrum'.*

Liatris (Asteraceae), gay feather

This summer-flowering bulbous plant can usually be found in between the permanent plants. It is a very good cut flower. The flower has the characteristic of opening from top to bottom. The bulbs can stay in well-drained soil; light cover is necessary.

L. spicata	purple-pink	July–Aug.	28 in (70 cm)
L. s. 'Floristan Violett'	violet	July–Aug.	36 in (90 cm)
L. s. 'Floristan Weiss'	white	July–Aug.	36 in (90 cm)
L. s. 'Kobold'	violet-mauve, sturdy	June–Sept.	20 in (50 cm)
L. s. 'Picador'	deep purple	July–Aug.	36 in (90 cm)

***Lilium* (Liliaceae), lily**

Give lilies well-drained soil and protect them against frost in the winter. Lilies like the cool ground between other plants where the sun does not shine on them and the flower stems are more sheltered against the wind.

The lilies listed here are reasonably winter-hardy. A great many hybrids are too, but to a lesser extent. Consult a current catalog with regard to these hybrids. Do not let the fleshy bulbs dry out. Initially keep them in damp peat or plant them straight away in March. Some bulbs produce roots only on the base of the bulb (*L. candidum*). These require shallow planting. Bulbs which also produce roots on the stem (far and away the most common) can be planted at an ordinary depth (4–8in/10–20cm). The depth also depends on the size

'Black Dragon' *trumpet lily.*

of the bulb. These lilies can all stay in the ground over winter, but I prefer to plant them in the spring, when they can start to grow immediately. They can stay in the ground the following winter and are less susceptible to the cold. The more botanical species are stronger and can be planted out equally in fall.

Propagate them by taking bulb scale cuttings. In the summer, when they are flowering, remove the outermost scales from the bulb and plant them out separately. They must be planted under glass at a temperature of over 68°F (20°C). After only a short time, bulbils start to grow on these scales. This plant has plenty to offer the enthusiast with a cold frame.

Trumpet lilies			
	L. 'African Queen'	orange	4 ft (1.2 m)
	L. 'Black Dragon'	white, purple outside	4 ft (1.2 m)
	L. 'Black Magic'	cream/purple-brown	4 ft (1.2 m)
	L. 'Golden Splendour'	orange-yellow	36 in (90 cm)
	L. 'Green Dragon'	greeny white	4 ft (1.2 m)
	L. 'Pink Perfection	pinky-mauve	5 ft (1.5 m)
	L. regale	cream/pink	5 ft (1.5 m)
	L. r. 'Album'	white/green	4 ft (1.2 m)
	L. 'Royal Gold'	yellow	4 ft (1.2 m)

Other lilies belonging to various groups:	*L.* 'Bright Star'	white with orange		28 in (70 cm)
	L. 'Connecticut'	yellow		32 in (80 cm)
	L. 'Enchantment'	orange-red	early	28 in (70 cm)
	L. 'Giganteum'	orange-yellow		6 ft (2 m)
	L. 'Imperial Gold'	white/yellow		4 ft (1.2 m)
	L. 'Journey's End'	pink/white		36 in (90 cm)
	L. 'Olivia'	white, pinky-red on outside		3 ft (1 m)
	L. 'Sterling Star'	white		32 in (80 cm)
Lilies for pots and garden:	*L.* 'Apollo'	cream, pink outside	Aug.	24 in (60 cm)
	L. 'Apeldoorn'	orange		
	L. 'Bright Star'	ivory white, apricot center		28 in (70 cm)
	L. 'Côte d'Azur'	soft pink	June–July	14 in (35 cm)
	L. 'Elvin's Son'	golden yellow	Aug.	12 in (30 cm)
	L. 'Enchantment'	orange		
	L. 'Harvest'	soft orange with specks		16 in (40 cm)
	L. 'Stargazer'	pink, white-specked		
	L. 'Red Carpet'	vivid red	June–July	16 in (40 cm)

Lilium *'Connecticut King'.*

Left: Nerine bowdenii *is a plant for warm climates or warm greenhouses.*

Right: Nerine undulata.

Mirabilis (Nyctaginaceae)

Like *Celosia*, this plant comes in vivid colors, which require care in combining with other colors. A separate flower-bed perhaps? The flowers do not open until midday and then give out a wonderful scent until the evening, which gives rise to the name of 'Tea Time' for a group of strains which are sold by color. Give them a sunny, warm site. If they dry out, they will die back too early. They are supplied only mixed. The tuber-like roots can be lifted to overwinter. Store them as for dahlias. It is a good plant for clay soil – it does not mind even heavy clay.

M. jalapa	mixed	July–Sept.	36 in (90 cm)

Nerine (Amaryllidaceae)

Like *Vallota* and *Zephyrantus*, this plant must be treated as a tub plant. Do not allow nerines to overwinter at less than 41°F (5°C); prevent them from drying out. The most suitable ones for the garden are *N. bowdenii* and *N. undulata*. Treat them as for *Canna* in cold climates; lift them in fall and plant them out again, but not too early. The flowering period of this species greatly depends on the temperature in the summer. They are often grown in greenhouses as cut flowers.

N. bowdenii	pink	Sept.–Oct.	20 in (50 cm)
N. flexuosa 'Alba'	white	Sept.–Oct.	16 in (40 cm)
N. hybr. 'Crispa'	pink, curly bloom	Sept.–Oct.	16 in (40 cm)
N. undulata	pink	Aug.–Sept.	16-20 in (40–50cm)

The natural color of Ornithogalum thyrsoides *is white. This cut flower often used to be sold dyed. Happily, dyeing flowers has gone out of fashion as the colors always look unnatural.*

***Nomocharis* (Liliaceae)**

This lily-like bulbous plant from China has rather flat flowers. It requires moisture-retentive, but above all humus-rich, soil in partial shade. Root damage is not good for it: rotting could be the result. Leave the bulb in the ground as it is fully frost-hardy. Snails can be a problem.

N. pardanthina	pale pink, purple specks	June–July	3 ft (1 m)
N. saluenensis	white or pink, purple specks	June–July	32 in (80 cm)

***Ornithogalum* (Liliaceae), chincherinchee**

They are often sold as bulbs in the spring, but they are not particularly suitable for the garden. It is better to plant them in tubs or pots on the patio. It is not worth the trouble of keeping the bulbs after flowering: flowering will be disappointing. The chincherinchee is often imported as a cut flower.

O. thyrsoides	white	16 in (40 cm)

***Polyanthes* (Agavaceae), tuberose**

This tuberous plant originally comes from Mexico. Small, tube-shaped flowers hang along the full length of a thin stem. It is a greenhouse plant in all but frost-free climates; the species are given under the chapter on bulbs for indoor temperatures. The fragrant flowers can be bought in shops as a cut flower in late summer.

***Ranunculus* (Ranunculaceae), turban buttercup**

A distinction must be made between Turkish and Persian turban buttercups. The former have to be planted in November-December and the latter in February-March; cover them with straw or peat. They can also be sown under glass in the latter half of September. Although there are many strains, they are usually supplied mixed. They are not suitable for heavy clay soil – mix them with sharp sand and peat. Well-drained humus-rich sandy soil is ideal. Plant the claw-like tuberous roots in March, to flower in June to August; then lift again in the fall. Like freesias, it is difficult to provide ideal garden conditions for this plant.

Turkish turban buttercups	*R.* 'Boule d'Or'	golden yellow	early
	R. 'Hercules'	white	
	R. 'Romano'	red	
	R. 'Merveilleuse'	copper-yellow	
French turban buttercups	*R.* 'Primrose Beauty'	yellow	
	R. 'Mathilde Christina'	white	
	R. 'Orange Queen'	orange	
	R. 'Veronica'	red	
Peony-flowered turban buttercups	*R.* 'Brilliant Star'	red	
	R. 'Champagne'	pale yellow	
	R. 'Flora'	crimson, black center	
	R. 'Golden Ball'	yellow	
Persian turban buttercups	*R.* 'Barbaroux'	red	
	R. 'Jaune Suprême'	yellow	

Ranunculus

Sparaxis. *They are not sufficiently winter-hardy; it is better to plant them in pots in cold climates and bring them in during a frosty spell.*

R. 'Fire Ball'	dark red
R. 'Pink Perfection'	pink

***Rhodohypoxis* (Liliaceae)**

This low-growing flowering plant with a fleshy rootstock is suitable for the rock garden. Swellings, which are produced on the root stock, can be propagated, although seed can also be sown. This summer-flowering plant comes from South Africa. Water it sufficiently during the growing and flowering period, but it prefers drier conditions in winter. So it is not easy! It is preferable to bring them inside from the end of September, so they do not also have to be given separate protection against frost. One final demand: they require acid soil.

R. baurii	various colors	July–Sept.	2 in (5 cm)
R. b. 'Alba'	white	July–Sept.	2 in (5 cm)
R. platypetala	white	June–Aug.	4 in (10 cm)

***Sparaxis* (Iridaceae)**

This old-fashioned plant has fallen out of favor, which could be due to its vivid colors. Like *Ixia*, this plant has a sword-shaped leaf; the flowers are in spikes. It is a good cut flower, originating from South Africa. Plant it in November, reasonably deep to prevent frost damage. Specially prepared corms can be bought in spring: these flower later than the stated months. Propagate by planting out the young cormlets again or use the bulbils from the leaf axils.

S. tricolor 'Fire King'	dark orange-red, black center

Tiger flowers are sold 'by color' or mixed. I don't know the variety name of this Tigridia.

S. t. 'Scarlet Glory'	red	May–June	12 in (30 cm)
S. t. 'Sulphur Queen'	soft sulfur yellow		

Tigridia (Iridaceae), tiger flower

This old-fashioned plant from Mexico has wrongly gone out of fashion. If well-protected with mulch, they can overwinter outside. After a few years, they will flower freely. Each bloom flowers separately for only one day, but there are so many to a stem that they appear to be flowering very well.

T. pavonia	mixed	July–Oct.	20 in (50 cm)
T. p. 'Alba'	white, red heart	July–Oct.	20 in (50 cm)

Tritonia

This plant does well in a cold, but frost-free greenhouse, or in the garden in frost-free sheltered areas. It is comes only mixed in colors ranging from yellow to orange.

T. crocata	mixed	June–July	10 in (25 cm)

Tropaeolum (Tropaeolaceae), climbing cherry

The tuberous plant *T. tuberosum* and the rhizomatous plant *T. speciosum* both come from South America. The former requires a warm, sunny site, but has no particular soil requirements. Plant it deep, at least 8 in (20 cm), and cover it well, particularly in the first few years to prevent frost damage. Let it grow through twigs or put up wire to give the long tendrils support. *T. speciosum* does well in partial shade on moist, humus-rich soil. It prefers cool summers.

T. tuberosum	orange/yellow	Aug.–Oct.	5 ft (1.5 m)
T. speciosum	reddish	July–Aug.	10 ft (3 m)

***Urginea* (Liliaceae), sea squill**

This bulbous plant is large, both in the circumference of the bulb and height of the flower (4 ft [1.2 m]), is not frost-hardy – and it's not the most beautiful, either! Plant the bulb in a sunny site in sandy soil, but water regularly during the growing period. In cold climates, lift the bulb at the same time as dahlias and treat it in a similar fashion in the winter. They are also suitable for a large pot, which can be put in a sunny site.

U. maritima	white	Aug.–Sept.	4 ft (1.2 m)

Vallota

This amaryllis-like plant can tolerate only a few degrees of frost. In cold climates, it is better to let it overwinter in a cool and frost-free site as a tub plant. Put it in pots on a warm site on the patio.

V. speciosa	orange-red	July	20 in (50 cm)

***Zephyranthes* (Liliaceae or Amaryllidaceae)**

Treat this plant as for *Vallota*. Only *Z. candida* can overwinter outside, provided it is well covered. The others must be kept in frost-free conditions (minimum 41°F [5°C]). The bulbs can be bought in fall in colder climates.

Z. candida	white	Sept.–Oct.	8 in (20 cm)
Z. grandiflora	bright pink	May–June	12 in (30 cm)
Z. rosea	pink	Sept.–Oct.	8 in (20 cm)

Zephyranthes grandiflora

Fall-Flowering Bulbous and Tuberous Plants

When the last tall summer-flowering plants such as *Crocosmia* and *Canna* are still in flower, the much lower-growing fall-flowering plants also begin to come to life again. In this way, the garden continues to look full of life.

Colchicum autumnale *'Waterlily' in mixed planting with the more refined* C. autumnale *'Album'.*

Despite the announcement that summer is really over now, we are still pleasantly surprised by the free-flowering crocus, saffron, and cyclamen. Apart from a few special small plants, these three account for most of the latest-flowering bulbous plants.

With the exception of the meadow saffron, fall-flowering bulbous plants can be obtained only from specialist bulb suppliers. The reason for this is the time when they are supplied: August–September. Only a few people go to a garden center then. Also, at that time, the garden is looking so splendid that it does not occur to most garden owners to start buying new plants. Fall-flowering bulbous plants are also not very easy, although they can stay in the ground; some winter protection is often needed. I hope that the following summary will lead to them becoming better-known and better-loved. You can place orders by post with most companies. Bulbs can be dispatched more easily than most other plants, but it is necessary to order the following plants in good time.

Colchicum (Liliaceae), meadow saffron

This king of the fall-flowering plants can be propagated simply by lifting the flowering plants and planting them out again separately from each other. This tuberous plant, which flowers in September, is also called a dry-flowering plant as it will flower without soil, on the window ledge, for example. This will not harm the plant if it is planted back in the garden immediately after flowering. It is difficult to give its

Anemone coronaria

height: the rather floppy flowers are 6-8 in (15-20 cm) high, but the shiny dark green foliage, which does not appear until the spring and which dies back again in June, is 16-20 in (40-60 cm) high. The meadow saffron is often wrongly confused with the fall crocus. The plant combines best with ground-cover plants such as galium and waldsteinia, and it can naturalize wonderfully between deciduous shrubs. At about the time when these plants begin to lose their looks, the colchicum starts to flower. They are often wrongly thought of as a shady plant: the flowers are more compact and sturdy in the sun. The plant is poisonous.

C. agrippinum	red-purple, speckled	Sept.–Oct.	4 in (10 cm)
C. autumnale	pale purple-pink	beg. Sept.	6 in (15 cm)
C. a. 'Album'	white	Aug.–Sept.	4 in (10 cm)
C. a. 'Album Plenum'	white, double	Aug.–Sept.	4 in (10 cm)
C. a. 'Roseum Plenum'	violet	Oct.	4–6 in (10–15 cm)
C. bornmuelleri	mauve, white center		8 in (20 cm)
C. byzantinum	purple-pink	Sept.	6 in (15 cm)
C. b. 'Album'	white	Sept.	6-8 in (15–20 cm)
C. cilicum	pale pink-violet	end Sept.	4 in (10 cm)
C. luteum	orange-yellow	Jan.–Mar.	4 in (10 cm)
C. hybr. 'Lilac Wonder'	violet with white stripes		8–10 in (20–25 cm)
C. h. 'Violet Queen'	purple, short stem		6 in (15 cm)
C. h. 'Waterlily'	pink-purple, double	Sept.–Oct.	6–8 in (15–20 cm)
C. speciosum	bright violet pink	Sept.–Oct.	6 in (15 cm)
C. s. 'Album'	white	Sept.–Oct.	6 in (15 cm)

***Crocus* (Iridaceae), crocus (fall-flowering)**

The first fall-flowering crocuses begin to flower in September; others (suitable for frost-free climates) do not flower until Christmas. In contrast to the spring-flowering members of their species, they flower at a time when other plants still have their leaves. Therefore put them in a separate site where they are well protected or (for the later-flowering varieties) where they can be seen from the house. *C. sativus* is the well-known saffron crocus, a must for every herb garden.

C. banaticus	purple-violet	Oct.–Nov.	
C. cartwrightianus 'Albus'	white		4 in (10 cm)
C. goulimyi	soft mauve		6 in (15 cm)
C. karduchorum	pale lavender/pink		4 in (10 cm)
C. laevigatus	mauve, scented	Dec.	
C. l. 'Fontenayi'	mauve, striped on outside	Nov.–Jan.	4 in (10 cm)
C. medius	violet-purple, orange stamens	Oct.	6 in (15 cm)
C. nudiflorus	deep purple	Oct.	4 in (10 cm)
C. pulchellus	pale mauve/violet stripes		4 in (10 cm)

C. p. 'Zephyr'	white, gray flush	Sept.–Oct.	3 in (8 cm)
C. sativus	mauve		4 in (10 cm)
C. speciosus	dark violet-blue	Sept.	6 in (15 cm)
C. s. 'Aitchisonii'	soft blue, darker on outside	Oct.	6 in (15 cm)
C. s. 'Artabir'	soft blue, darker stripes	Sept.–Oct.	6 in (15 cm)
C. s. 'Conqueror'	sky-blue	Sept.–Oct.	4 in (10 cm)
C. s. 'Oxonian'	violet-blue, large	Sept.–Oct.	6 in (15 cm)

***Cyclamen* (Primulaceae), cyclamen**

This well-known indoor plant is still too little known as a garden plant and yet it is not difficult. Sowing is even rather easy: direct onto the intended site. After years in the same place it will reward you with a sea of flowers. When buying the bulbs, make sure that they have come from a nursery and have not been stolen from the wild (Turkey or Greece)! This is an ideal rock garden plant. *C. coum* flowers in spring, but, if mild, may flower from January. *C. cilicium* is not fully winter-hardy. Cover the corms with a few inches (centimeters) of loose soil. *C. persicum* (the ancestor of our room cyclamens) is an exception to this; this corm likes to stay on the surface. *C. hederifolium* is the best propagator and even likes heavy clay soil. The less winter-hardy species (*C. africanum, C. balearicum, C. graecum, C. libanoticum, C. pseudibericum, C. rohlfsianum,* and

Fall crocuses between green and falling leaves look totally different from their spring brothers, which are surrounded by bare ground.

C. trochopteranthum) are not included in the following list.

C. cilicium	pinky-red	Sept.–Nov.	2 in (5 cm)
C. coum	pinky-purple	Dec.–Mar.	2 in (5 cm)
C. cyprium	white/deep red specks		3 in (8 cm)
C. hederifolium (C. neapolitanum)	pink	Sept.–Nov.	4 in (10 cm)
C.h. 'Album'	white	Sept.–Nov.	4 in (10 cm)
C. intaminatum	soft pink, miniature plant		
C. mirabile	pale pink (expensive) Oct.		
C. persicum	white/pink sheen	Dec.–Mar.	2 in (5 cm)
C. pseudibrium	purple-crimson	March	
C. purpurascens (C. europeaum)	pink, strong-scented	June–Sept.	4 in (10 cm)
C. repandum	crimson	April–May	

***Galanthus* (Liliaceae), fall snowdrop**

This snowdrop, which flowers from fall through to the spring, depending on the climate, is for a warmer site in the garden. The flowering period depends on the weather conditions. It can be obtained only from specialist companies. Give this snowdrop a warmer, sunnier, and drier site than the species mentioned under the spring-flowering bulbs.

G. reginae-olgae	white	Nov.–March	8 in (20 cm)

Cyclamen hederifolium *begins to flower well after a number of years on the same site.*

Sternbergia lutea *is the most commonly planted fall bulb after crocus and meadow saffron. The plant can also go on the window ledge.*

***Leucojum* (Liliaceae), 'fall snowflake'**

Although it is not official, this plant should be called the "fall snowflake." It is a smaller version of the summer snowflake, a small rare plant, for a moist, sunny site in the rock garden.

L. autumnale	white	Sept.–Oct.	4 in (10 cm)

***Scilla* (Liliaceae)**

An exception amongst the scillas is the following special species from South and Central Europe, a relatively small garden plant with short clusters of flowers from which six to twenty small flowers hang. This plant makes a good combination with *Leucojum*.

S. autumnalis	pale to dark violet	Aug.–Sept.	4 in (10 cm)

***Sternbergia* (Liliaceae)**

S. lutea is one of the few fall-flowering bulbous plants and the best. It is widespread in the wild in the Mediterranean region. Plant it in a sunny site where the soil is well warmed by the sun. Although it has long been cultivated, *S. clusiana* is less well known. This plant likes warmer conditions. The foliage appears in the spring. They can also be planted in pots and are even suitable for growing indoors.

S. clusiana	greeny yellow	Oct.–Nov.	10 in (25 cm)
S. colchiciflora	soft yellow, small	Oct.	4 in (10 cm)
S. fisheriana	yellow	Oct.	4 in (10 cm)
S. lutea	yellow	Sept.–Nov.	6 in (15 cm)
S. sicula	golden yellow	Oct.	4 in (10 cm)

Tulipa *'Princess Irene'*

Bulbs for the Home and the Greenhouse

Nearly all the plants listed below belong to the "old-fashioned" house plants. After the introduction of central heating, they mostly disappeared from the range as they cannot tolerate well the dry, warm air.

Small-flowered tuberous begonias are at their prettiest in the home.

Many plants could not stand up to the higher temperatures and lower air humidity that have resulted from central heating, especially in those regions where the winters are usually very cold and very dry. Bulbous plants have a period in which they die back, after which they must be stored, a nuisance in confined spaces.

Plants are also very much subject to fashion. A number of plants are making a comeback, but due to increasing prosperity, we no longer think twice about throwing away a plant once it has flowered. The cyclamen is an example of this, as are the rechsteineria and the achimenes.

There is not much point in mentioning the plants that are found only in botanical gardens and are not widely grown. Although the plants in this chapter are all grown or sold commercially, some are also difficult to get hold of. Moreover, bulbous plants must be bought only when they are dormant so the periods they are available are restricted. Some of the plants mentioned here can also be bought in full flower in a pot. But even these are sold during a limited period of the year.

Achimenes (Gesneriaceae)

Put this plant from tropical South America in a warm site and do not let it overwinter at temperatures of less than 50°F (10°F). Water it only with lukewarm water. It can be propagated by breaking the rhizomes into pieces during the dormant period, but also by taking cuttings and growing them in a warm room.

A. erecta	red, sometimes striped	July–Sept.	16 in (40 cm)

	A. grandiflora	purple-red	24 in (60 cm)
	A. patens	violet, very hairy plant	6 in (15 cm)
Hybrid cultivars	A. 'Ambroise Verschaffelt'	white, violet-veined	
	A. 'Camille Brozzoni'	purple, white eye	
	A. 'Little Beauty'	pink, small flower	
	A. 'Paul Arnold'	purple, large flower	
	A. 'Purple King'	purple	

Begonia (Begoniaceae), tuberous begonia

In the past, tuberous begonias were often used as house plants. The small-flowered varieties are particularly suitable for this. They are plants which will reward you with a window ledge full of flowers all summer long. The most suitable variety for this is *B. bertinii*, although the pendulas (with hanging flowers) and multifloras are also suitable.

B. bertinii	orange-red
B. b. 'Compacta'	orange-red, compact
B. multiflora 'Flamboyant'	red, small-flowered
B. 'Helene Harms'	yellow, small-flowered
B. 'Mme Richard Galle'	orange, small-flowered
B. pendula	all colors

The Achimenes *hybrid is one of the easiest bulbous plants for the home.*

Left: Cyclamen with frilled flowers.

Right: Cyclamen persicum. *This wild cyclamen is the ancestor of all strains for room cultivation.*

***Canna* (Cannaceae), Indian shot**

This plant comes from tropical America. The smaller cannas are suitable for growing in a room. All cannas will, moreover, stay somewhat smaller in a pot than in a warm nutrient-rich site in the garden (see chapter 7).

C. indica 'Golden Lucifer'	silver yellow	24 in (60 cm)
C. 'Lucifer'	red, yellow edge	24 in (60 cm)

***Cyclamen* (Primulaceae), cyclamen**

Along with the begonia, azalea, and fuchsia, cyclamen are the most important pot plants. Cyclamen is also grown as a cut flower. The stems of this plant are 16 in (40 cm) long. *C. persicum* and its descendants are grown as house plants. When buying, pay attention to the quality: the leaf stalks must be sturdy. Put your hand on the leaf with the flower stems between your fingers; when you rotate everything, the pot (even an earthenware pot!), together with the soil, should be able to hang by the leaf stems.

When caring for the plant, water only with lukewarm water. Pour the water on the edge around the bulb and not in the saucer: the result of the latter is that all the salts stay on the top of the pot due to evaporation, which makes root growth impossible. By pouring water on top, the nourishing salts are better distributed throughout the entire potting medium. If you do not throw the cyclamen away after flowering, allow it to overwinter in a cool place (46 to 50°F) (8 to

Oxalis triangularis is usually sold as a house plant.

10°C) after flowering. The plant can be put outside from mid-May. There are a great many strains, which are divided into groups.

Smooth-edged strains The petals are not incised. Most strains come within this group.

Frilled strains The petals are finely incised.

Rococo forms The petals are spread out horizontally and are frilled.

Cristata forms Flowers with an eye; the frills are a different color from the rest of the bloom.

Double-flowered strains These are feathered with a crest on the petals.

Victoria forms These are cyclamen which have thicker flower stems and a double set of petals.

Small-flowered varieties This scented cyclamen came about by crossing botanical cyclamen with large-flowered cyclamen.

Left: Unlike the Paperwhites, Narcissus *'Tête-à-Tête' requires a cool forcing period.*

Right: Haemanthus multiflorus *has a prettier bloom than* H. albiflos.

***Cyrtanthus* (Liliaceae)**

The species of this relatively little-known cut flower from South Africa described below grow fairly low. Allow them to overwinter at temperatures above 50°F (10°C). After flowering in the spring, they can be planted out in a warm site, but bring them in again at the end of September. This bulbous plant can be propagated by seed.

C. parviflorus	orange-yellow	12 in (30 cm)

***Hymenocallus* (Liliaceae), spider lily**

This plant needs to be treated in the same way as *Hippeastrum* and *Haemanthus*, also with regard to propagation. It must overwinter at a reasonably warm temperature: minimum 60°F (15°C). Let the plant stay in the pot during the dormant season: the foliage does not have to die back. Do not feed during this period and water sparingly. The plant can be placed in a warm site outside in summer (see also chapter 7).

H. longipetala	cream	March–April	3 ft (1 m)

***Eucharis* (Liliaceae)**

This luxury plant is more suitable for the warm greenhouse in proper soil with an artificially heated floor. Growth is stunted when cultivated in pots. The blooms of this "flattened narcissus" are often used in wedding bouquets. They are suitable only for the experienced amateur gardener.

E. grandiflora	white	spring/fall	28 in (70 cm)

Haemanthus (Liliaceae), red Cape lily

The *Haemanthus* genus comprises roughly fifty species, which are native to equatorial and south South Africa. Although the leaf is thicker and fleshier, it resembles the clivia. They need a similar treatment, although they like even drier conditions in the winter. Let them overwinter in a cool bedroom; the plant can be moved to a warm room again in the spring. In the summer it can go in a shady site on the patio.

H. albiflos	whitish
H. a. var. *pubescens*	as above, with hairy foliage
H. multiflorus	red
H. m. 'Superbus'	deep red

x _Hippearelia_ (Liliaceae)

This bulbous plant is sold as a bulb, but also often as a pot plant. This hybrid between the *Hippeastrum* and *Sprekelia* genera requires a warm sunny site on the window ledge. Treatment is similar to that of the amaryllis.

x *Hippearelia*	red	Feb.–March	12 in (30 cm)

Hippeastrum (Liliaceae), amaryllis

The present cultured forms have arisen from crosses between botanical species from South America. Professional growers grow this plant as a cut flower; it is grown as a pot plant to a limited extent and is then usually sold as a bulb. Only a few of the seventy-five species are grown. The well-known hybrid cultivars have come about by crossing a number of these species.

Do not make the mistake of putting the bulbs in the ground in the garden in the summer: the soil there is too cold. More ground warmth is required for the plant to grow well and to store food for the coming flowering period. Oversummer them in the pot in a warm room or in a cold frame. Let them die back in September by stopping watering. In January they can be potted up again and left in the room, where the flower stems will quickly start to grow again. Anyone can get this bulb to flower again and even to propagate itself by means of planting out the young offsets separately. Do not throw away the bulbs when they have finished flowering. Remember that during their growing period the bulbs need warmth.

Hybrid cultivars

H. 'Apple Blossom'	soft pink, white striped, green center
H. 'Candy Cane'	bright red, white striped
H. 'Dutch Belle'	silver pink
H. 'Lady Jane'	orange-pink, double
H. 'Minerva'	vivid red, white stripe
H. 'Mont Blanc'	silver white
H. 'Picottee'	white, fine red edge
H. 'President Johnson'	silver white, fine red edge, green center
H. 'Purple Sensation'	purple-pink
H. 'Red Lion'	scarlet red
H. 'Rosy Queen'	bright pink, paler near the center

H. 'The First'	reddish-orange, cream center
H. gracilis 'Donau'	soft pink
H. g. 'Pamela'	warm red
H. g. 'Germa'	yellow, darker center
H. g. 'Spotty'	green pinky-red striped, spotted petals

***Lachenalia* (Liliaceae), Cape cowslip, leopard lily**

Plant a few bulbs of this plant from South Africa in a pot in September and put them away somewhere cool. As growth progresses, they like more water, after which they can be put in a room when the stems are being produced. They can be propagated by planting out the young bulblets and by sowing seed. If grown from seed, the bulbs will produce flowers again after three years.

L. aloides	yellow, green tip	March-April
L. a. 'Nelsonii'	yellow, with green stripe	March–April
L. bulbifera	orange-red, green stripe	Dec.–Jan.

***Lilium* (Liliaceae), lily**

Low-growing species and varieties of lily are also sold as pot plants. After flowering, these lilies can be planted out in the garden, where they can then be grown as a garden plant and will flower again the following year.

Sinningia *hybr. with double flowers.*

Pot lilies The lilies known as American hybrids have upright blooms and are sturdy. Most are not tall and are therefore the most suitable for indoors.

L. 'Apollo'	cream, pink outside	Aug.	24 in (60 cm)
L. 'Apeldoorn'	orange		4 ft (1.2 m)
L. 'Côte d'Azur'	soft pink	June–July	14 in (35 cm)
L. 'Elvin's Son'	golden yellow	Aug.	12 in (30 cm)
L. 'Enchantment'	orange		
L. 'Golden Melody'	yellow		
L. 'Harvest'	soft orange with speckles		16 in (40 cm)
L. 'Prominence'			
L. 'Stargazer'	pink, speckled white		
L. 'Red Carpet'	vivid red	June–July	16 in (40 cm)

***Moraea* (Iridaceae), butterfly iris** This easy-to-grow plant is suitable for the frost-free greenhouse or out in the garden in warmer climates. It is native to South Africa. It flowers profusely on split stems. Keep the dormant corms warm.

M. ramosissima	yellow, tip with brown specks	April–May	24 in (60 cm)

***Narcissus* (Amaryllidaceae), narcissus** Most narcissi must be kept in a cool, dark place before they can be moved into a room. The varieties listed below are the easiest to grow. Plant the bulbs and put them straight into light and into the room. The entire growing process will then follow. They can be densely planted in bowls filled with gravel or sand. Take care that the bulbs are not standing in water, but are just above it. After flowering, the bulbs can be thrown away: they are not suitable for garden use.

N. 'Soleil d'Or'	golden yellow		16 in (40 cm)
N. 'Paperwhite'	white		16 in (40 cm)

***Notholirion* (Liliaceae)** This bulb for the cold greenhouse or a cool room can also be put in the most sheltered site in the garden, with good protection against frost.

N. thomsonianum	pale violet-pink	May–June	28 in (70 cm)

***Oxalis* (Oxalidaceae), wood sorrel, lucky clover** In the spring, give *oxalis* fresh potting medium. Store the tubers or swollen roots in a reasonably warm place and pot them up in February. Do not put outside until the weather is dependably warm. For room culture, put them in a site which is not too warm and which is protected against direct sunlight. For garden use, *Oxalis deppei* can be treated as the dahlia: pot it in April and lift it in October.

O. lasiandra	pinky-violet	4 in (10 cm)
O. regnellii	green foliage, white flower	
O. rubra	green foliage, pinky-red flower	
O. triangularis	dark red foliage	
O. t. 'Mijke'	dark foliage, bright pink flower	
O. t. 'Alba'	green foliage, white flower	
O. vulcanicola	yellow	

***Proiphys* (Liliaceae)** This little-known plant, which has long been cultivated in botanical gardens, comes from Malaysia, which means that the soil temperature must be reasonably high: about 68°F (20°C). The dry bulb should also overwinter in a warm place. Apart from that, treat the bulb the same way as for amaryllis.

P. amboinensis	snow white	spring	20 in (50 cm)

***Rechsteineria* (Gesneriaceae)** *Gesneria* used to be the scientific name and is now also used as the common name.

Let them overwinter in a cool place, a bedroom, for example, or another room where the central heating is not turned on. Pot them up in fresh potting medium in February, after which they can go straight into a warm room again. It is a strong plant, but you will probably not get it to flower as prettily as with a bought plant.

R. cardinalis	vivid red	May–June	10 in (25 cm)

***Sandersonia* (Liliaceae)** Put this lily-like plant with shiny foliage and hanging bells on long stems in a room or reasonably warm greenhouse. In the summer it can possibly go in a warm, sunny site in the garden.

It can overwinter in a cold greenhouse, provided it is also well-covered.

S. aurantiaca	orange-yellow	summer	30 in (75 cm)

Tulbaghia violacea. *Although the flowers look pretty here, they are usually surrounded by foliage which smells disturbingly of onions.*

Sinningia (Gesneriaceae), gloxinia

This old-fashioned house plant needs indirect light (no sun) and a warm room with a high humidity. Do not spray: this creates spots on the flowers and leaves.

Overwinter at temperatures above 50°F (15°C), and put it in a warm room again from February. Always give it lukewarm water. If it does not get enough water, the leaf shrivels up and looks ugly or gets brown edges; if it gets too much water, the stem can rot, with the result that the whole plant will eventually collapse. The present-day strains are hybrid products from botanical species from Brazil.

Sinningia hybrids	red, pink, violet, blue
S. 'Kaiser Friedrich'	red/white
S. 'Kaiser Wilhelm'	blue/white
S. 'Violacea'	blue
S. 'Roi des Rouges'	red
S. 'Mont Blanc'	white
S. 'Switzerland'	dark red, white edge
S. 'Tigrina Red'	speckled red

For improved flowering, do not repot the Vallota.

Sprekelia (Liliaceae), Jacobean lily, Aztec lily

Do not plant this bulbous plant from Central America too deep: the nose of the bulb should protrude slightly above the soil. Although they can be planted outside in a warm site in the summer, these bulbs are nevertheless more suitable for room culture. Let them overwinter in a warm place: minimum 54°F (12°C). Apart from that, they are treated in the same way as the *Hippeastrum*. They can be propagated by detaching and planting out the offsets from the parent plant, or by sowing seed. A few years will go by before the plants will flower again and sometimes it does not happen at all, despite being well cared for.

S. formosissima	dark red	June	12 in (30 cm)

Zantedeschia aethiopica, *the traditional house plant.*

***Tulbaghia* (Liliaceae)**

Even without flowers, this plant looks attractive and rather like grass, with a gray-green waxy sheen on the leaf. It is a good cut flower and can be recognized by its onion scent. Botanists differ as to whether this plant should be counted as a member of the lily family or the onion family. It can be grown both in the home and greenhouse and on the patio. As far as I know, there is no bulbous plant with a longer flowering period.

T. violacea	pink, small flower	May–Oct.	16 in (40 cm)

***Vallota* (Liliaceae), Scarborough lily**

Allow this plant, which resembles the amaryllis, but with smaller flowers, to overwinter in a cool and dry place, but leave it in the pot. In the summer, indoors is the best place, but it can also go outside in good weather. As a cut flower, the flowers can be cut even when in bud: they will open out fully.

V. speciosa	orange-red	June–July	16 in (40 cm)
V. s. 'Major'	red	June–July	16 in (40 cm)
V. s. 'Alba'	white	June–July	16 in (40 cm)

***Veltheimia* (Liliaceae), winter red hot poker**

The blooms of this bulbous plant from South Africa resemble our red hot poker perennial plant. Put them in a cool place in winter. When the leaves have died back in the spring, they can be put outside in the summer. They are propagated by seed. As with the hyacinth, young bulblets are produced if the bulb base is hollowed out before planting.

V. capensis	yellow, red specks	Jan.–April	16 in (40 cm)
V. glauca	red, yellow specks	Jan.–April	16 in (40 cm)

***Zantedeschia* (Araceae), arum lily, calla lily**

The spathes of the flowers are of great ornamental value. The species, also known as richardia and calla, all come from tropical Africa. Repot the plant in the spring and put it indoors in a cool, light position. From mid-May to mid-October, the plants can go outside in light shade. Keep sufficiently moist and feed throughout the growing and flowering period. Give them a lot of water when they come into leaf. Propagate by dividing the fleshy rhizomes.

Z. aethiopica	white	32 in (80 cm)
Z. a. 'Childsiana'	white, compact plant	16 in (40 cm)
Z. a. 'Green Goddess'	green, white center	32 in (80 cm)
Z. elliottiana	yellow	32 in (80 cm)
Z. rehmannii	white, deep purple inside flower	28 in (70 cm)
Z. r. 'Carminea'	pink-purple-pink	16 in (40 cm)

next page: Zantedeschia rehmannii *'Carminea'.*

Bulbs for Indoor Temperatures

It seems a bit out of fashion, but even indoors, on the window-ledge, flowering bulbs can produce a beautiful display. This tradition should be restored to its rightful place.

The small narcissi all lend themselves to being forced indoors. Narcissi from the Jonquilla *group merit their preferred position because of their scent. The photo shows the small-flowered* Narcissus *'Rip van Winkle'.*

Bulbs which ordinarily are intended for the garden but which can temporarily be enjoyed in the room form a separate group in this book. The easiest of these are those known as dry-flowerers, such as the meadow saffron and *Sauromatum*, which can flower, without a pot or any soil, dry on the window ledge. Some need temperature treatment in order to flower indoors.

In other words, we cannot describe these plants simply as garden plants, house plants, or tub plants. For optimal flowering, the flowering bulbs for indoors must be large. After their flowering period, all these bulbs can be planted out in the garden, where they will usually require an extra year to regain the strength required to bring them to flower. Hyacinths, tulips, and tuberoses are best thrown away after flowering indoors; any subsequent flowering in the garden will be disappointing and it is not worth the trouble of planting them out.

At my grandparents' house, in spring, the window ledges were always full of containers, bowls, and glasses of bulbs. Among my friends, I have not come across anyone who still lets spring bulbs flower in the home. This may be due to the present-day hurried life-style, or perhaps we find flowering bulbs old-fashioned.

Nostalgia or not: bulbs for growing indoors belong in a book on bulbous plants.

With grape hyacinths, you do not have to look at just one bulb: they are one of the cheapest bulbs. Start them individually before growing them together to achieve this result.

Tulip vases, hyacinth glasses, and crocus pots

Over the centuries, special features were made for bulbs or their flowers so that they could be better enjoyed indoors. An example of this is the tulip vase, also called the flower pagoda or staggered vase, which is designed for cut tulips and other cut flowers. The ornamental vases have a number of small spouts, which will hold only one or two flowers. They became particularly popular in Persia at the beginning of the seventeenth century. From there, they appeared in Italy and then in the Netherlands.

Mary, wife of King William III of Great Britain, was mad about gardens, flowers, Chinese porcelain and Delft pottery. She is said to have been the great impetus behind the development of the tulip vase. The vases, with Chinese, Egyptian, Oriental, and Dutch influences, were made in Delft. At Hampton Court, William and Mary's palace, where they lived during their reign, some of these vases were over 5 ft (1.5 m) tall. After the beginning of the eighteenth century, these vases disappeared again, but today reproductions of these old vases are being made. The old ones can be found only in museums, where they are worth looking at even without flowers. Avant-garde designs made by present-day artists are giving the tulip vase a new lease of life.

Hyacinth and crocus glasses are also old. The older ones are made from colored glass. The early, expertly made glasses of thin glass are prettier than the thick factory models produced later, which can be recognized from the seams that run over the glass. The plastic models

in which the bulb is held between three lips in the lid are not suitable for use: when the bulb grows and the heavy clusters of flowers develop, the small vases are too light and topple over.
Crocus glasses have the same design as the old hyacinth glasses, but are much smaller. As far as I know, they are no longer made. Crocus pots, which hold roughly ten crocus corms, often used to be shaped like a small tree trunk. The porcelain or pottery pots also have holes in the side, through which the bulb noses can be made to protrude. Spherical designs appeared later, which can now be found only made of plastic.

Grape hyacinth Shallow bowls are the most suitable for grape hyacinths. Put them in a cool and dark position until the noses of the bulb are 2 in (5 cm) long. Then bring them into the light, though even then a room is still too warm. It is better to enjoy them in a cool bedroom.

Cyclamen Winter-hardy cyclamen grow best in clay soil, where they will flower freely after a few years. The small-flowered open-ground varieties can also be grown in pots. In this case, use the garden soil in which they were growing and heel them in on a shady site, a little job for August. When they begin to flower, they can be brought inside. Flat, low bowls are the prettiest, as the low-growing dainty flowers look better in them.

Left: Hyacinthus *'Blue Jacket'.*

Right: This Chionodoxa *'Pink Giant' is not the only one suitable for forcing into flower. The earliest low-growing spring-flowering plants can nearly all be forced.*

Left: Hyacinthus *'Anne Marie'.*

Right: Crocus *'Jeanne d'Arc' is the best-known large-flowered white crocus.*

Meadow saffron

Meadow saffron is the easiest bulb for room culture. Buy the bulbs in August and simply put them dry on the window ledge. They will then flower all on their own without soil or water! Immediately after flowering, plant them outside at a depth of 3 in (8 cm). When choosing the site, take into account that the foliage which will come up in the spring will be 20 in (50 cm) high.

Chionodoxa

This plant flowers early anyway, so forcing is not necessary. Plant them in pots, heel these in in the garden, and bring them indoors in February. After a couple of weeks they will come into flower in the room.

Hyacinth: growing in glasses

In October, put the (prepared) bulbs in the glasses. Fill the glasses with water right up to the base of the bulbs and top up each week. Put the glasses in as cool a position as possible, but definitely frost-free and dark. When the noses are almost 4 in (10 cm) high, they can be put into the warmth and light. If the bulbs are put into the light too soon, the flower buds will be stunted, while the leaves carry on growing. Buy new bulbs for forcing each year to avoid disappointment. Unprepared bulbs can also be put in glasses, but the chance of failure is much greater. Do not put these bulbs in glasses after mid-September.

Hyacinth: pot culture

Prepared hyacinths can be put straight indoors in a cool position. They will flower earlier than the other members of their species for the garden. These bulbs have already been temperature-treated. When the shoot is 3 in (8 cm) long, they can be put in a warm room. If the bulbs are intended to flower for Christmas, they will have to already have been planted in pots in September. Do not forget to water them now and again. This can easily be forgotten if they are left in an out-of-the-way spot. The pale blue 'Delft Blue' strain is the best for room culture.

Spike hyacinths

When the prepared hyacinths have produced a spike of approximately 3 in (8 cm), they can be put in the light. If growers have pre-grown the hyacinths, they are sold as spike hyacinths in a pot. There is nothing more for you to do, as they can be put on the window ledge as they are.

Multiflora hyacinths

The multifloras are not suitable for glasses. They will not fit in because of the shape of the bulb. These bulbs, which flower with several stems at a time, can be planted three or five together in a bowl. Bring them into the warmth when the noses are 3 in (8 cm) long.

Crocus

Special crocus pots with holes in the sides through which the crocuses can flower are on the market. Shallow earthenware bowls or flower dishes are also good.

Culture

Plant the crocuses in September at the latest. Fill the bowl with 1.5 in (4 cm) potting compost or river sand and heel it in in the garden. Cover well with straw or peat to protect against hard frosts. In mid-January, bring the bowls inside and put them in a cool room, but in good light. The buds will appear quickly. It is also possible to keep the bowls inside in a cool, frost-free place, in a cool, dark cupboard, for example. Do not forget to water them from time to time. These bowls can also be put in a light position in mid-January. With the exception of the yellow ones, all large-flowered crocuses are suitable. When buying the bulbs, take care to get large-sized ones.

Narcissus

The 'Paperwhite' narcissi are well-known for indoor forcing. Along with the meadow saffron, these are the easiest bulbs for room culture, where nothing can go wrong. Plant the bulbs in a layer of gravel, so that they will stay upright even when the stems are tall. When watering, take care to ensure that the bulbs stay just above the water level to prevent rotting. Give more water as the foliage develops and evaporation increases. They can be put in a light position straight away, but do not put them in a warm room until the flower buds have formed. Ordinary garden narcissi are also suitable for flowering in the room. These prefer not to be put directly in the light, and in order to prevent the flower buds from drying out, regular spraying with water is also necessary. Although the effect is not pretty, plastic bags can be put over the plants to prevent the buds from drying out too soon.

Left: Although the pot and flower color of this Narcissus *'Paperwhite' match each other well, for me there is nothing better than a red earthenware pot with matching saucer.*

Right: Narcissus *'Hawera' is suitable both for the rock garden and for a shallow bowl in the room.*

Sauromatum

Like the meadow saffron, this bulb can also be made to flower without water or soil: simply put it on the window ledge. This "dry-flowering" plant must be planted out in the garden immediately after flowering in the room.

Although the plant is recommended as a good flowerer in the room, the flower's carrion smell is horrible. You will probably prefer to grow it in pots on the patio. In winter, store the corms in a dry and frost-free place and plant them up again in February for flowering in April. The plant can be obtained without any particular difficulty, sometimes simply on the market. It is a pity that the name of *Arum cornutum* for this plant still persists, since the correct name has for years been *Sauromatum venosum*. The flower is purple-brown and approximately 8 in (20 cm) high. The light green foliage which appears later reaches a height of 32 in (80 cm).

Siberian squill

Only the low-growing *Scilla sibirica* is appropriate for growing indoors. It is quite an easy plant; heel in outside and take out of the ground again in February or March. They will soon be in flower inside. After flowering, the bulblets can be planted out in the lawn, for example.

Glory of the snow

Glory of the snow does not lend itself to being forced in warmer temperatures.

It can be planted in pots which are then heeled in in the garden. At the beginning of February, when the flowers are in bud, the pots with the bulbs can be brought inside. Put them in a cool place indoors.

Sternbergia Plant this fall-flowering plant with bright yellow flowers in pots in August/September immediately after purchase. They can be put into a warm room immediately.
After flowering, they can be planted out in the garden. They are easy to grow provided they are planted early enough.

Tuberose The scientific name is *Polianthes*, belonging to the Agavaceae, previously to the Amaryllidaceae. This old-fashioned house plant used to be grown for wedding bouquets. I know this bulb only from folklore literature and culture descriptions. I never come across it in more recent cut-flower handbooks. The *P. tuberosa* species from Mexico was the most cultivated species. The bulbs can be obtained only from the genuine specialist. In the old book *The Garden for Expert and Amateur,* I read the following about this plant: "The flowering period can be extended by planting the bulbs at different times: February planting gives flowers in July; with bulbs planted in April you can expect flowers from September. The bulbs are annuals. As they do not propagate well in pots, it is advisable to buy new ones each year. Put the bulbs into the warm immediately: at least 60°F (15°

Left: the Siberian squill is quite low-growing: it is displayed to better advantage in a shallow bowl rather than a deep pot.

Right: Glory of the snow is also an early-flowering plant under natural conditions in the garden.

C), preferably warmer. It is possible to plant them out in a warm site in the summer. In that case, plant them by a patio where the wafts of scent will take you by surprise." Although classed with the bulbs for the home in this book, this plant must not go back to the cool garden after flowering, but straight to the warmth of a warm greenhouse. It is therefore easier to buy fresh bulbs each year.

Polyanthes geminiflora	green flower	July–Aug.	
P. tuberosa	waxy-white	May or Sept.	32 in to 3 ft (80 cm to 1 m)
P. t. 'Excelsior Pearl'	white		

Tulip Pots 6 in (15 cm) in diameter are suitable for tulip culture indoors. Plant the bulbs in ordinary potting compost in October. Heel the pots in in a well-drained site in the garden. There must be about 4 in (10 cm) between the surface of the soil and the top of the pot. Cover the ground with a thick layer of peat or straw, so that the pots can be removed from the ground even in frosty conditions (not before mid-January). Put them in a cool position inside only when the noses are at least 3 in (8 cm) high. They then like to be in a warm room.

The lighter the conditions into which they are put, the shorter the flower stem will remain. Before putting it on the window ledge, wait until the flower stem is almost 6 in (15 cm) long. Instead of being in pots in the garden, they can also overwinter indoors. In that case, the temperature during the period when the roots are being formed must definitely not be above 55°F (13°C). Do not forget to keep the soil moist throughout. The following varieties are suitable for room culture:

Single-flowered:		
T. 'Bellona'	silver yellow	16 in (40 cm)
T. 'Christmas Marvel'	bright red	14 in (35 cm)
T. 'Couleur Cardinal'	dark red	14 in (35 cm)
T. 'Generaal de Wet'	orange with yellow	16 in (40 cm)
Double-flowered:		
T. 'Carlton'	deep scarlet	10 in (25 cm)
T. 'Monte Carlo'	lemon yellow	12 in (30 cm)
T. 'Peach Blossom'	deep pink	12 in (30 cm)
T. 'Schoonoord'	snow white	12 in (30 cm)
Triumph tulips:		
T. 'Bing Crosby'	shiny red	16 in (40 cm)
T. 'Fidelio'	salmon pink	20 in (50 cm)
T. 'Lucky Strike'	deep red, yellow edge	16 in (40 cm)

Index

Boldface indicates photographs
Italicized names indicate a Plant Family